EAT
TO STAY
YOUNG

EAT
TO STAY
YOUNG

INGREDIENTS & RECIPES
TO REJUVENATE YOUR BODY & MIND

GILL PAUL
NUTRITIONIST: KAREN SULLIVAN, ASET, VTCT, BSC

hamlyn

An Hachette UK Company
www.hachette.co.uk

First published in Great Britain in 2016 by Hamlyn,
a division of Octopus Publishing Group Ltd
Carmelite House
50 Victoria Embankment
London EC4Y 0DZ

Distributed in the US by
Hachette Book Group
1290 Avenue of the Americas
4th and 5th Floors
New York, NY 10020

Distributed in Canada by
Canadian Manda Group
664 Annette Street
Toronto, Ontario, Canada M6S 2C8

ISBN 978-0-600-63085-2

Printed and bound in China

10 9 8 7 6 5 4 3 2 1

All reasonable care has been taken in the preparation
of this book but the information it contains is not
intended to take the place of treatment by a qualified
medical practitioner.

This book includes dishes made with nuts and nut
derivatives. It is advisable for those with known
allergic reactions to nuts and nut derivatives and those
who may be potentially vulnerable to these allergies
to avoid dishes made with nuts and nut oils. It is also
prudent to check the labels of prepared ingredients
for the possible inclusion of nut derivatives.

Ovens and broilers should be preheated to the
specified temperature—if using a convection oven,
follow the manufacturer's instructions for adjusting
the time and temperature.

Medium eggs should be used unless otherwise stated.

Some of the recipes in this book have previously
appeared in other titles published by Hamlyn.

Assistant Editor: Meri Pentikäinen
Art Director: Jonathan Christie
**Photographic Art Direction, Prop Styling
and Design:** Isabel de Cordova
Photography: Will Heap
Food Styling: Annie Nichols
Picture Library Manager: Jen Veall
Assistant Production Manager: Caroline Alberti

CONTENTS

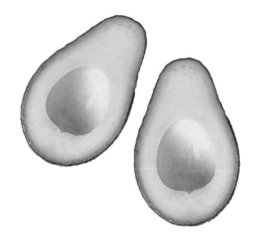

6   Introduction

PART I

10   **Young superfoods**
Your key ingredients

26   **What's your problem?**
At-a-glance problem solver

30   **Putting it all together**
Weekly menu planner

PART II

Young recipes
36   Breakfast
50   Snacks
70   Lunch
92   Dinner
112   Desserts

126   Resources
127   Index
128   Acknowledgments

INTRODUCTION

There are plenty of anti-aging treatments on offer, each more extreme than the other, for those who are desperate enough to try them. There are bee-sting and snake-venom facials. You can cover yourself in leeches to detoxify your blood or apply bull's sperm for thinning hair. You can choose from countless surgical procedures to lift, tuck, and rearrange your face and body.

However, common sense says that the most effective way to slow the aging process is to treat your cells from within by giving them all the nutrients that they need to maintain their youthful functions. And the best way to do that is through the food we eat.

How we age

Our organs, our bones, and other tissues in our bodies go through a number of changes as we age. Cells start to die more frequently and the mechanisms to replace them don't work as efficiently as they used to when we were younger.

Free radicals, the natural waste products of the process by which oxygen from the air and glucose from the food we eat are used to produce energy, are a major cause of aging. In most young people, free radicals are quickly mopped up and disposed of but, as we age, they are not dealt with so readily, and an unhealthy lifestyle can create many more, which can kill off the healthy cells or cause them to mutate into cancerous ones.

The rate at which we age

Part of what affects the rate at which we age is genetic—our predisposition to disease and to the outward signs of aging come from our parents.

Part is simply due to the amount of wear and tear our bodies receive over time. But a significant part of how well we weather the aging process is determined by the way we live our lives.

A poor diet, too much alcohol, smoking, stress, pollution, and sunbathing all hasten the degeneration of tissues. A balanced diet full of delicious anti-aging nutrients and a healthy lifestyle, on the other hand, will keep you biologically younger for longer.

Your weight in middle age

- It's easy for excess weight to creep up as the metabolism slows in middle age, particularly for people with sedentary lifestyles. Those who are plump tend to get fewer wrinkles than their lighter friends because there is a thicker layer of fat under their skin. However, there the advantages end because the extra strain on the heart and the circulatory system, bones, and joints, are likely to give those who are overweight more health problems.

- Weight-loss diets in your 40s or 50s can be very aging, both externally, with wrinkles and pouches of loose skin seemingly appearing overnight, and internally as essential nutrients are leached out of bones, muscles, and organs. The solution lies in eating a balanced diet containing all the anti-aging superfoods, and leading an active life, with at least an hour of exercise a day. Aim to include both aerobic exercise (the kind that makes you out of breath, like running) and muscle-strengthening exercise (such as yoga, tai chi, or Pilates).

How to eat to stay young

1. Choose whole foods!

Modern processing methods remove a lot of the goodness from our foods and replace it instead with sugars, chemical additives, and preservatives. The most important rule for eating to look and feel younger is to buy natural, whole ingredients and always cook or prepare them from scratch. That way you will be getting optimum benefits from every last mouthful.

2. Appreciate antioxidants

Foods containing the antioxidant vitamins A, C, and E, the mineral selenium, as well as a range of phytonutrients, such as lycopene, are the front line of our defense against free radicals and also form a core part of the *Eat to Stay Young* diet. Fruits and vegetables contain useful antioxidants, and you should aim to eat a wide range of different types. A key tip to remember is that the brighter the colors and the fresher they are, the better they'll do their job.

3. Opt for omegas

Omega-3 fatty acids have several anti-aging benefits. They keep blood cholesterol levels healthy, preventing heart disease; they keep the joints supple and prevent inflammation; they keep the brain agile and can ward off memory loss; and they are also nature's own moisturizer for skin and hair. You'll find them in oily fish (sardines, salmon, mackerel, and tuna are good sources), as well as olive oil, nuts, and seeds.

4. Fill up with fiber

Our digestive systems can slow down as we age, leading to constipation and inefficient absorption of nutrients. Eating plenty of insoluble fiber (found in whole grains and vegetables) adds bulk to food waste and helps to speed its passage through your digestive system. Always choose unrefined carbohydrates, including brown rice and whole-grain bread and cereals.

Soluble fiber is also important. It forms a kind of gel with water in the digestive trait and slows down the absorption of sugars into the blood, so it makes us feel full for longer and prevents blood-sugar fluctuations. Some good sources of soluble fiber are oats, lentils, carrots, and all kinds of berries.

5. Keep your bones strong

A good night's sleep makes everything look better the next day, and it is also essential for regulating hormones, maintaining a healthy blood pressure, balancing mood, improving energy levels, and keeping the immune system strong. Magnesium, calcium, and certain amino acids aid restful sleep and you'll find them in abundance in the recipes in this book.

6. Choose B vitamins

B vitamins support the nervous system, helping us to relax and cope with stress, as well as maintaining our metabolic rate and keeping energy levels up. Vitamin B_6 helps with mood and stops premature graying of the hair, while B_{12} helps stop shrinkage of the brain. Good sources of protein are essential for providing these B vitamins, and include lean meats, poultry, fish, eggs, and legumes, as well as dairy products.

7. Cut the bad habits

You may have got away with puffing on cigarettes, sipping cocktails, sunbathing, and living on fast food and takeout in your twenties, but the damage will mount as the years go by. No miracle cream or radical potion will be able to undo it.

Getting started

For many, the biggest lifestyle change may be starting to cook from scratch. It takes a little longer to cook a meal from raw ingredients, but none of the recipes in this book is complicated and many can be thrown together in fewer than 10 minutes. It could be the wisest investment of time you ever make—and you'll find that food bills shrink when you're not paying for fancy packaging and glitzy marketing campaigns.

For all-round good health, and to look and feel younger on every level, follow the two-week meal planner on pages 30–33. To address specific symptoms of aging, such as wrinkles or thinning hair, see the problem solver on pages 26–29. On pages 12–25 you'll find a list of the powerhouse anti-aging superfoods, along with a number of ways you can introduce them into your regular diet. Try them all, and drink loads of water throughout the day to keep your system well hydrated.

At the age of 20, we have the health and appearance we inherited; at 50 and beyond, we have the face and body we have created through our own life choices. Be sure you make wise choices. Even though you may not be able to turn back the clock, you can look and feel as though you have.

YOUNG
SUPERFOODS

SUPERFOODS

Eaten regularly, these multifunctional foods will have noticeable rejuvenating effects on the whole body, both inside and out.

Brazil nuts

✔ Raise energy levels and lift mood
✔ Improve memory
✔ Encourage healthy skin, hair, and nails
✔ Promote heart health
✔ Reduce degenerative effects of aging
✔ Aid virility and libido
✔ Increase metabolism

Rich in healthy fats, Brazil nuts are full of selenium, an antioxidant mineral. They also have chemicals that reduce inflammation, slowing down age-related degeneration.

They are rich in...

→ Selenium, which balances mood, slows down skin- and hair-aging, repairs cell damage, and improves elasticity
→ Vitamin E, for healthy skin and hair, lower cholesterol and reduced risk of heart attack and stroke
→ Zinc, needed for memory, virility, and collagen formation in the skin and joints
→ B vitamins, which enhance metabolism, mood, energy, heart health, skin and hair health, and lower cholesterol levels

Use in... salads with feta cheese, grapes, and mixed greens; dip into dark chocolate; grind with fresh tarragon, Parmesan cheese, and olive oil for pesto; fruit or vegetable crisp toppings; muesli; chop finely and sprinkle over squash or carrot soups; puréed in fresh fruit and yogurt smoothies.

SEE: FRUIT & NUT MUESLI, P42; BERRY & BRAZIL NUT SMOOTHIE, P39; SPICY BRAZIL NUTS, P56.

Cranberries

✔ Prevent tooth decay and gum disease
✔ Protect against heart disease
✔ Improve short-term memory
✔ Reduce inflammation and cellulite
✔ Encourage brain and digestive health
✔ Balance blood sugar

Rich in antioxidants, which slow down the effects of aging and improve heart and dental health, cranberries also aid short-term memory and reduce urinary-tract infections. Highly fibrous, cranberries regulate nutrient absorption, digestion, and blood sugar.

They are rich in...

→ Proanthocyanidins (PACs), which stop bacteria from sticking to the surface of teeth and gums (and the urinary tract), reducing the risk of infection and decay

→ Flavonoids, to help prevent heart disease, including atherosclerosis, reduce signs of aging, and ease muscle and joint pain

→ Phytonutrients, which protect the heart, teeth, and gums, reduce high blood pressure, and prevent stomach ulcers

→ Vitamins A and C, which moisturize the skin, promote collagen, and fight free radicals that can cause wrinkles and environmental damage to the skin

→ Chemicals that prevent stomach ulcers

Use in... smoothies; tagines or other chicken, turkey, or pork dishes; chutneys; porridge or muesli; snack with nuts and seeds; stuffings; oat bars, fruit crisps, or muffins; couscous; dried in a green salad with goat cheese; juice; baked apple stuffing with almonds, cinnamon, and brown sugar.

SEE: CRANBERRY MUFFINS, P69; SPICED RAISIN & CRANBERRY COOKIES, P64; BROCCOLI SALAD WITH DILL & PINE NUTS, P76; CRANBERRY ICE CREAM WITH DARK CHOCOLATE, P118.

Tuna

✔ Improves heart health
✔ Lifts mood and beats fatigue
✔ Lowers blood pressure and cholesterol
✔ Balances blood sugar
✔ Promotes healing and repair of cells
✔ Lowers risk of dementia and aids memory
✔ Keeps joints supple
✔ Improves skin and hair quality
✔ Protects eyesight

The omega-3 oils in tuna help prevent the degeneration of cells from hair, skin, and nails to brain, joints, and heart. Tuna is rich in cell-renewing proteins, as well as nutrients that lower cholesterol and blood pressure, and even ensure a good night's sleep.

It's rich in...

→ Selenium, which protects the body from free-radical damage and helps support healthy liver and brain function

→ Omega-3 oils, for heart and brain health, better memory and mood, reduced inflammation, and lower risk of obesity and macular degeneration

→ B vitamins, for improved sleep, and red blood cell health to increase energy, and lower the risk of atherosclerosis

→ Vitamin D, to build and maintain strong bones and teeth, and prevent diabetes

Use in... salad Niçoise; grill tuna kebabs with a citrus marinade; brown rice salad with bell peppers, scallions, diced tomatoes, and chickpeas; on baked potatoes or toasted rye bread with fat-free Greek yogurt, fresh dill and black beans; sushi; form into burgers; grilled on a whole-wheat bun; spread with pesto and roast until just cooked.

SEE: TOASTED QUINOA, TUNA & LENTIL SALAD, P98; SESAME-CRUSTED TUNA WITH GINGER DRESSING, P102; TUNA WITH PEPPERS & FENNEL GRATIN, P104.

Eggplant

- ✔ Encourages heart and eye health
- ✔ Balances blood sugar
- ✔ Lowers blood pressure and cholesterol
- ✔ Enhances memory
- ✔ Promotes healthy digestion
- ✔ Encourages stronger, healthier hair
- ✔ Eases fatigue
- ✔ Helps angina
- ✔ Discourages cellulite

Eggplants are low in calories, high in fiber, and bursting with nutrients, such as vitamins A, B, and C (essential for great skin, hair, eyesight, and mood). They also contain potassium, magnesium, phosphorus, and calcium, which aid bone and brain health.

They are rich in...

- → Nasunin, which protects the fats in brain cells for optimum brain function and helps produce collagen in the skin
- → Chlorogenic acid, which reduces bad cholesterol, improves circulation, slows down the degenerative effects of aging, and aids heart health
- → Fiber, to balance blood sugar, promote digestion, discourage cellulite, and help protect against type-2 diabetes
- → Potassium, to lower blood pressure, ease angina, and lift energy levels and mood

Use in... vegetable curries; ratatouille; brush slices with olive oil, pepper, and basil and grill; roast whole and purée flesh with lemon juice, salt, cumin, and a little live yogurt as a dip or spread for flatbreads or toast; thinly sliced instead of pasta in lasagne; stuff with ricotta cheese, mint, oregano, and spinach.

SEE: SMOKY EGGPLANT DIP, P53; EGGPLANT & SESAME NOODLE SALAD, P70; MISO EGGPLANT WITH RICE NOODLES, P100; EGGPLANT, CHICKPEA & PANEER CURRY, P110.

Olive oil

- ✔ Lowers cholesterol and blood pressure
- ✔ Promotes brain health
- ✔ Reduces wrinkles and improves skin
- ✔ Protects against memory loss and cognitive decline
- ✔ Supports cardiovascular and bone health
- ✔ Lifts mood and relieves pain
- ✔ Helps prevent obesity

Olive oil protects against cardiovascular disease and lowers the risk of stroke and heart attacks, while its anti-inflammatory properties reduce pain, support the joints, and slow down age-related degeneration. It's rich in antioxidants, and studies have also found that it protects against osteoporosis.

It's rich in...

- → Polyphenols, which are antioxidants that help stop age-related disease and degeneration, and reduce inflammation
- → Monounsaturated fats, which reduce the risk of heart disease and promote skin health (including a reduction in wrinkles), act as anti-inflammatories, and prevent cognitive decline
- → Vitamin E, which improves skin texture and elasticity, and acts as an antioxidant to protect the body from free radicals
- → Vitamin K, for a healthy nervous system, good brain function, and strong bones and teeth

Use in... stir-fries; drizzle over toast in place of butter or margarine; salad dressing with fresh and dried herbs and lemon juice; bake into crisp, herby flatbreads or biscotti; as the basis for sweet polenta or pistachio cakes; to flavor steamed vegetables and pastas; instead of butter in pastry.

SEE: VIRTUALLY EVERY SALAD DRESSING AND COOKED SAVORY DISH IN THIS BOOK.

Red bell peppers

- ✔ Promote healthy eyesight
- ✔ Make skin more elastic
- ✔ Speed up the metabolism
- ✔ Encourage heart health
- ✔ Lower blood pressure
- ✔ Aid digestion
- ✔ Lower cholesterol

With a wide range of nutrients that encourage health and well-being on all levels, red bell peppers are rich in vitamin C, which is essential for hair health, eyesight, energy levels, and the joints, skin, and nails. They also contain silicon, which improves the condition of hair and nails, and magnesium and vitamin B_6, which enhance mood, relaxation, and healthy sleep patterns, and combat premature graying. Bell peppers are also full of antioxidants, which help delay the signs of aging.

They are rich in...

- → Lycopene, which encourages elasticity in the skin and stimulates collagen production, while supporting healthy heart function
- → Vitamin A, which supports healthy eyesight, and lutein, which lowers the risk of macular degeneration and cataracts
- → Potassium, to lower blood pressure, prevent angina, encourage the health of the brain and nervous system, and raise mood
- → Vitamin C, which is an excellent antioxidant that also supports the health of skin and joints, and prevents premature graying

Use in... ratatouille with eggplant, zucchini, and tomatoes; stuff with herbs, brown rice, and feta cheese and roast; slice and eat raw with hummus or other dips; roast and serve in sandwiches with hummus or halloumi; slice and add to quiches, omelets, or scrambled eggs; roast and purée with herbs for a yummy pasta or pizza sauce.

SEE: BROCCOLI & RED PEPPER FRITTATA, P46; MEDITERRANEAN STUFFED BELL PEPPERS, P82; TUNA WITH BELL PEPPERS & FENNEL GRATIN, P104; HEARTY RATATOUILLE, P108.

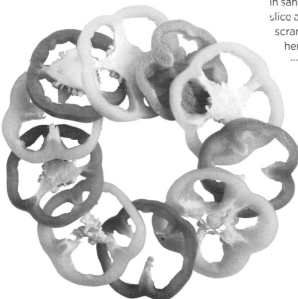

Tomatoes

- ✔ Protect the skin and bones
- ✔ Reduce the risk of cancers, arthritis, and joint problems
- ✔ Lower cholesterol
- ✔ Encourage heart health and eyesight

Tomatoes will provide you with a burst of vitamins, minerals, and other elements that promote the faster growth of new cells, including cells in the skin.

They are rich in...

- → Lycopene, which protects the skin from sunburn and UV rays and promotes the formation and renewal of collagen; also important to protect against cancer, heart disease, and osteoporosis
- → Phytonutrients, which lower cholesterol and prevent atherosclerosis
- → Vitamin C, for the production of collagen required for healthy hair and skin; it also reduces the risk of arthritis, macular degeneration, and joint problems
- → Biotin, which is necessary for healthy skin and hair, and critical for cell turnover and heart health; adequate amounts in the diet can prevent prematurely gray hair

Use in... pasta sauces; casseroles, stews, and soups; roast and top with oregano, olive oil, and a sprinkling of pecorino; sundried in sandwiches and salads; topping for bruschetta, baked feta, or foil-cooked white fish; salad with red onions and basil; cherry tomatoes as a snack; juices with celery salt and lemon.

SEE: HUEVOS RANCHEROS, P48; BROCCOLI & RED PEPPER FRITTATA, P46; MEDITERRANEAN STUFFED PEPPERS, P82; AVOCADO & TOMATO TOSTADOS, P60; BRUSCHETTA WITH TOMATOES & BASIL, P62; GAZPACHO, P83; HEARTY RATATOUILLE, P108.

Pomegranates

- ✔ Encourage healthy digestion and elimination
- ✔ Balance weight and blood sugar
- ✔ Lift mood
- ✔ Regulate blood pressure
- ✔ Preserve collagen in skin
- ✔ Promote heart and eye health
- ✔ Lower cholesterol
- ✔ Regenerate cartilage in joints
- ✔ Prevent hair loss

Pomegranate seeds and the bitter white pith contain key antioxidants to reverse signs of aging. They also increase oxygen levels to the heart, encourage moist, supple skin, aid symptoms of inflammatory conditions, such as arthritis, and strengthen hair follicles, preventing loss of hair.

They are rich in...

- → Fiber to balance weight and blood-sugar levels, promote digestion, and ease constipation
- → Folic acid, for a healthy nervous system and reduced inflammation
- → Punicalagin, which lowers blood pressure and cholesterol, and reduces the risk of angina and atherosclerosis
- → Vitamin K and manganese for bone health

Use in... fresh, fruity salsas served with tagines, pork, or lamb dishes; smoothies with berries and live yogurt; breakfast cereals and muesli; on top of quartered pears with goat cheese; nutty wild rice or quinoa salads; the juice to glaze ribs, sprinkled with the seeds.

SEE: BLUEBERRY POMEGRANATE SMOOTHIE, P36; FRUIT SALSA & CINNAMON TRIANGLES, P114; CARROT & BEET TABBOULEH, P78; BROCCOLI SALAD WITH DILL & PINE NUTS, P76; GUAVA-GLAZED PORK TENDERLOIN, P96; POMEGRANATE PANNA COTTA, P122.

Watercress

- ✔ Prevents bone loss
- ✔ Lowers blood pressure
- ✔ Stabilizes heart rate
- ✔ Supports health of skin and hair
- ✔ Required for cardiovascular health
- ✔ Boosts libido
- ✔ Fights fatigue
- ✔ Encourages healthy gums
- ✔ Enhances digestion

With more calcium than milk, more vitamin C than most fruits, and plenty of iron, this peppery vegetable improves digestive function, boosts energy levels, encourages healthy eyesight, and has been used over the centuries to improve libido. It's also high in fiber, which can balance blood-sugar levels and improve digestion.

It's rich in...
- → Vitamin K, which can help prevent memory loss and encourage the health of bones and teeth
- → Vitamin C for healthy skin, hair, connective tissues, and gums, as well as improving immunity
- → Vitamin A for healthy skin and eyes, reducing the risk of macular degeneration and cataracts, as well as preventing night blindness
- → Flavonoids, such as lutein, zeaxanthin, and carotene, which promote vision and cardiovascular health

Use in... sandwiches instead of lettuce; in salads with avocado; braise with garlic and lemon; use instead of spinach in stuffed pasta dishes; blend with apples for a nourishing smoothie; use as a base for pesto instead of basil; simmer with leeks and stock, then purée for a light soup; add to lightly cooked omelets or frittatas with goat cheese.

SEE: WATERCRESS SOUP WITH CHEESE AND OAT CRACKERS, P88; BROCCOLI SALAD WITH DILL & PINE NUTS, P76.

Carrots

- ✔ Boost liver function
- ✔ Ease constipation
- ✔ Lower cholesterol
- ✔ Support heart and bone health
- ✔ Boost immunity and metabolism
- ✔ Promote healthy eyesight
- ✔ Reduce wrinkles, age spots, and dry skin
- ✔ Promote strong, healthy hair
- ✔ Raise libido

Carrots stimulate liver function, which helps digestion, hormone balance, and energy levels. High in fiber, they aid elimination and are full of nutrients that stop bloating.

They are rich in...

- → Fiber, which lowers cholesterol, balances blood sugar, and helps healthy digestion
- → Vitamins C and E, to aid circulation to the scalp, which encourages hair growth and prevents premature graying
- → Antioxidants and polyacetylenes, to protect the heart
- → Beta-carotene, which improves skin, heart, and liver health, and converts in the retina to rhodopsin, needed for night vision and prevention of cataracts and macular degeneration
- → Vitamin K, for a healthy nervous system, bone health, and brain function

Use in... stews; casseroles; soups; juices; salads; raw with guacamole, hummus, or other dips; roast with thyme, lemon, and olive oil; soup with orange zest; grated, add to cake; roast and add to sandwiches.

SEE: CARROT & LENTIL MUFFINS, P66; CARROT CHIPS WITH HONEY YOGURT DIP, P58; CARROT, CILANTRO & LENTIL SOUP, P91; CARROT & BEET TABBOULEH, P78; CARROT & PUY LENTIL SALAD, P75.

Fennel

- ✔ Improves digestion and eases constipation
- ✔ Lowers cholesterol and blood pressure
- ✔ Enhances brain function
- ✔ Protects eyesight
- ✔ Encourages heart health
- ✔ Prevents inflammation
- ✔ Balances mood
- ✔ Improves hair and skin
- ✔ Discourages cellulite

Fennel is a versatile vegetable that can be prepared in a wide variety of ways. It is a treasure trove of nutrients, and even half a bulb will supply good levels of vitamins A, B, and C, fiber, potassium, folic acid, manganese, phosphorus, calcium, iron, and copper.

It's rich in...

→ Iron and histidine, which encourage the supply of oxygenated blood throughout the body, improving brain, heart, skin, and hair health

→ Antioxidants, such as vitamin C and the amino acid arginine, which prevent macular degeneration and other age-related eye problems

→ Potassium, which facilitates connections within the brain and also lowers blood pressure and the risk of angina, raises energy levels, lifts mood, and regulates heartbeat

→ Fiber, to balance blood-sugar levels, promote healthy digestion and assimilation of nutrients, and prevent constipation, while discouraging cellulite

→ Sulfur and amino acids, to encourage healthy hair and skin

Use in... stews, soups, and casseroles; slice thinly in salads or serve as a crudité with dips; roast with a medley of other vegetables in a little olive oil, lemon juice, and black pepper; steam, braise, or sauté as an accompaniment; juice with apples or carrots; roast and purée with potatoes or other root vegetables.

SEE: CITRUS OLIVES, P50; FENNEL & CUMIN WALDORF SALAD, P74; FENNEL & MUSHROOM TARTS, P86; CARAMELIZED GARLIC TART, P106; HEARTY RATATOUILLE, P108; FENNEL-ROASTED LAMB WITH FIGS, P94; TUNA WITH BELL PEPPERS & FENNEL GRATIN, P104.

Oats

✔ Nourish the nervous system
✔ Balance blood-sugar levels
✔ Enhance memory and energy levels
✔ Encourage healthy digestion
✔ Promote restful sleep
✔ Lower cholesterol and blood pressure
✔ Lift mood, energy, and libido

Rich in vitamins, fiber, and a wealth of other nutrients, such as healthy fatty acids and protein, oats are particularly beneficial for their impact on the brain and digestion.

They are rich in...

→ Zinc, which is needed for immunity, libido, energy levels, memory, and collagen formation in the skin and joints

→ B vitamins, to promote a healthy nervous system, aid restful sleep, balance mood, and encourage healthy skin and hair

→ Soluble and insoluble fiber, to improve digestive health and the absorption of nutrients from food, and to balance blood sugar and cholesterol

→ Avenanthramides, antioxidants that help prevent cardiovascular disease

Use in... oatmeal, homemade muesli, and baked breakfast goods; use as a topping for crisps and sweet and savory pies; enjoy in oat bars and cookies as healthy snacks; use as a coating for baked fish or chicken; use in homemade soda bread; toast and toss with fresh fruit, herbs, and leafy salad greens for a crunchy salad; sprinkle on soups, stews, and casseroles.

SEE: FRUIT & NUT MUESLI, P42; BERRY & COCONUT PORRIDGE, P43; ON-THE-GO GRANOLA BARS, P40; BANANA, OAT & BLACKBERRY MUFFINS, P68; ROSEMARY OAT CRACKERS, P63; WATERCRESS SOUP WITH OAT CRACKERS, P88.

Cinnamon

- ✔ Lowers blood-sugar levels
- ✔ Supports liver function
- ✔ Boosts metabolism
- ✔ Lowers cholesterol
- ✔ Decreases memory loss and enhances brain activity
- ✔ Improves circulation
- ✔ Reduces joint pain
- ✔ Reduces the risk of tooth decay and gum disease
- ✔ Helps prevent bone loss
- ✔ Eases palpitations
- ✔ Raises libido
- ✔ Discourages cellulite

Just a little cinnamon, eaten daily, can play a strong role in preventing many of the problems that accompany aging, including reducing inflammation that can affect the heart, skin, brain, and joints. It helps to normalize blood-sugar levels, which play a role in excess weight and diabetes, and also has a calming effect that can encourage restful sleep and even ease palpitations. Its antibacterial properties help ensure good oral health.

It's rich in...

- → Polyphenols, antioxidants that promote heart health and lower the risk of cardiovascular disease, as well as reducing inflammation
- → MCHP (methylhydroxychalcone polymer) which enhances the effect of insulin, reduces blood sugar, lowers cholesterol, and encourages a sense of calm
- → Sulfur, which supports the liver to improve digestion and energy levels, while discouraging cellulite
- → Manganese to build bones, blood, and other connective tissues; it also contains a chemical that stops bones from breaking down
- → Calcium, which encourages restful sleep, and supports bone health and a healthy nervous system

Use in... oatmeal; stir into warm, freshly pressed apple juice; add to tagines, chili, and stews to bring out the flavor; use to flavor unsweetened fruit purées and serve with live yogurt; sprinkle over mashed bananas or puréed apples and pears and use as a spread; stir-fry with chickpeas steep cinnamon sticks in boiling water to make a nutritious, stimulating tea.

SEE: BERRY & BRAZIL NUT SMOOTHIE, P39; ON-THE-GO GRANOLA BARS, P40; CARROT CHIPS WITH HONEY YOGURT DIP, P58; BANANA, OAT & BLACKBERRY MUFFINS, P68; CARROT & BEET TABBOULEH, P78; CHICKEN MOLE, P92; GUAVA-GLAZED PORK TENDERLOIN, P96; BAKED HONEY, CARDAMOM & CINNAMON FIGS, P112; FRUIT SALSA & CINNAMON TRIANGLES, P114; CRANBERRY ICE CREAM WITH DARK CHOCOLATE, P118.

Blackberries

✔ Help digestion and ease constipation
✔ Balance blood-sugar levels
✔ Relieve pain and protect eyesight
✔ Promote healthy liver function
✔ Improve mood, memory, and libido
✔ Strengthen bones and teeth
✔ Protect against cardiovascular disease
✔ Discourage cellulite

Blackberries are full of age-defying anti-oxidants. They fight inflammation, while the high fiber content promotes healthy digestion and lowers cholesterol and blood pressure.

They are rich in...

→ Folate, to fight cardiovascular disease and memory loss; to produce serotonin for good mood and healthy sleep
→ Anthocyanins, which ease inflammation and improve circulation, muscle tone, and brain function
→ Fiber, to balance blood sugar and help digestion and liver function, which will discourage cellulite
→ Vitamin K, which is needed for the nervous system, brain function, and strong bones and teeth
→ Vitamin C, to prevent arthritis, macular degeneration, and joint problems, and produce collagen for better hair and skin

Use in... salads with walnuts, apples, and feta cheese; baking, such as muffins, scones, and fruit breads; fruit compotes and crisps; smoothies with almond milk and honey; roast with pork or duck; braise with red cabbage or fennel.

SEE: BERRY & COCONUT OATMEAL, P43; BANANA, OAT & BLACKBERRY MUFFINS, P68; BLACKBERRY BRÛLÉES, P123; APPLE & BLACKBERRY COMPOTE WITH ALMOND SCONES, P124; GUAVA ICE CREAM WITH BLACKBERRY COULIS, P120.

Broccoli

✔ Protects eyesight
✔ Reduces memory loss
✔ Supports bone health
✔ Boosts production of red blood cells
✔ Raises energy levels
✔ Supports liver function
✔ Protects against heart disease
✔ Reduces inflammation and cellulite
✔ Improves digestion

Rich in A, B-complex, C, and K vitamins, iron, zinc, phosphorus, calcium, potassium, and protein, broccoli has anti-inflammatory properties and fiber to stabilize blood sugar. It may even help reverse the effects of aging.

It's rich in...

→ Sulforaphane, which protects against cancer and free-radical damage in hair, bones, skin, heart, and joints, and improves blood pressure
→ Folate and calcium, for bone health and restful sleep, and to combat cognitive decline
→ Lignans, to fight cancers and heart disease, boost immunity, and brain health
→ Carotenoids, which support eye and heart health

Use in... stir-fries with scallions and light soy sauce; lightly steamed or raw florets in salads; add to the final cooking stage of soups, stews, and casseroles; frittatas and omelets; raw with healthy dips, such as guacamole and hummus; steam and purée with pine nuts, pecorino cheese, lemon juice, and olive oil for pesto.

SEE: PESTO BROCCOLI WITH POACHED EGGS, P80; BROCCOLI & RED PEPPER FRITTATA, P46; TOASTED QUINOA, TUNA & LENTIL SALAD, P98; BROCCOLI SALAD WITH DILL & PINE NUTS, P76; BUTTERNUT, BROCCOLI & MUSHROOM GRATIN, P105.

Sardines

✔ Help prevent blindness
✔ Strengthen bones and ease joint pain
✔ Support cardiovascular health
✔ Improve memory and ward off some forms of dementia
✔ Reduce wrinkles and thinning of skin
✔ Lift mood

Sardines are a great source of omega-3 fatty acids, which have many anti-aging benefits, such as the health of the heart and brain. Their other nutrients include vitamin D, essential for strong bones and teeth.

They are rich in...

→ Vitamin B_{12}, which is needed for healthy circulation, energy, and heart health
→ Vitamin D for strong bones and teeth, and the prevention of osteoporosis; also aids the absorption of calcium
→ Phosphorus, a mineral required to strengthen the bone matrix
→ Vital omega-3 oils, which maintain heart health, reduce mental decline, prevent degeneration of the eyes, reduce wrinkles by improving elasticity, ease inflammation, and restore luster to hair
→ Selenium, a renowned anti-aging mineral, which also helps lift mood

Use in... salads with cucumber, romaine lettuce, and feta cheese; grill or barbecue sprinkled with fresh herbs, lemon, and olive oil; mash into tomato pasta sauces; top with chopped fresh tomatoes, basil, and toasted pine nuts; crush on whole-grain crackers or rye bread and sprinkle with lemon juice and black pepper; marinate in fresh herbs, garlic, and saffron, and grill or broil.

SEE: ROASTED CHILE & LEMON SARDINES, P84; AVOCADO & SARDINE SALAD WITH ZESTY DRESSING, P72.

Dark chocolate

✔ Lifts mood, energy, and alertness
✔ Encourages relaxation
✔ Reduces pain
✔ Lowers blood pressure and cholesterol
✔ Balances blood sugar
✔ Reduces wrinkles and dry skin
✔ Prevents tooth decay
✔ Enhances brain and heart health
✔ Helps angina

The nutrients in dark chocolate work to slow the aging process on all levels, lift mood, improve alertness and relaxation, and contain chemicals to fight tooth decay. Its resveratrol can increase the life span of cells by up to 80 percent. Choose chocolate with at least 70 percent cocoa solids.

It's rich in...

→ Theobromine, which combats fatigue, boosts brain power, mildly stimulates the heart, and lowers blood pressure
→ Procyanidins, to relax blood vessels and aid circulation, heart health, and virility
→ Polyphenols, which lower cholesterol
→ Flavonoids, which reduce inflammation of the skin caused by exposure to UV light, and also increase circulation to the skin, making it moister, more supple, and less wrinkled
→ Copper, to help hair keep its color

Use in... spicy chili and curries to deepen flavor; melted in smoothies with banana and live yogurt; grate over oatmeal, fresh fruit, or yogurt; snack on a handful of chocolate-covered Brazil nuts; eat a couple of small squares as an after-dinner treat.

SEE: CHICKEN MOLE, P92; BANANAS WITH SPICED CHOCOLATE, P116; MOLTEN CHOCOLATE LAVA CAKES, P115; CRANBERRY ICE CREAM WITH DARK CHOCOLATE, P118.

Avocados

✔ Reduce inflammation and age spots
✔ Prevent wrinkles, dry skin, and dry hair
✔ Boost collagen production
✔ Encourage heart and brain health
✔ Lower cholesterol and blood sugar
✔ Improve digestion
✔ Promote healthy sleep and relaxation

A source of good fats, avocados are packed with nutrients that can improve heart and brain health, encourage relaxation, memory, and healthy sleep, ease pain, and slow the degeneration of hair, skin, and joints.

They are rich in...
→ Oleic acid, which increases good cholesterol and lowers bad cholesterol
→ Potassium, which protects the heart, circulatory system, and nervous system, reduces the risk of high blood pressure, angina, and stroke, raises energy levels and mood, and reduces pain and inflammation
→ Omega 3 fatty acids for heart, brain, and skin health
→ Magnesium, to promote healthy sleep and relaxation and boost immunity
→ Vitamins A and C, which slow down the effects of aging, maintain eyesight, and boost collagen formation in the skin

Use in... salads with tomato and mozzarella; mash on toast instead of butter, or in sandwiches instead of mayonnaise; guacamole with fresh crudités; warm and cold salads, or serve with a dressing on top; puréed in smoothies with vanilla, live yogurt, and honey.

SEE: BAKED AVOCADO EGG CUPS, P44; AVOCADO & TOMATO TOSTADOS, P60; CHILLED AVOCADO SOUP, P90; AVOCADO & SARDINE SALAD WITH ZESTY DRESSING, P72.

Guavas

✔ Balance weight
✔ Ease constipation and encourage healthy digestion
✔ Enhance brain function
✔ Improve skin quality and eyesight
✔ Lower blood pressure and cholesterol
✔ Prevent gum disease

This nutritious Asian fruit is bursting with protein to help repair and restore tissues in the body. With no cholesterol, few calories, and little sugar, it's ideal for a healthy diet. Its astringent and antibacterial compounds help prevent gum disease and tooth decay.

They are rich in...
→ Antioxidants and phenols, which protect against heart disease and stroke
→ Prebiotics and fiber, to encourage healthy digestion
→ Potassium, to ease palpitations and lower blood pressure
→ Vitamin C, to improve immunity, heart health, eyes, and skin
→ B vitamins, for relaxation, increased energy, and improved sleep
→ Vitamin A, for eye health, and reduced risk of cataracts and macular degeneration

Use in... smoothies with berries and bananas; stir into live yogurt and top with cinnamon and a swirl of maple syrup; use in juices with fresh vegetables and fruits; add to salads with feta cheese, chicken, and nuts; toss into curries and tagines; chop with mango in fresh salsas; or simply eat fresh and ripe as a snack.

SEE: GUAVA & GINGER SMOOTHIE, P38; GUAVA & MANGO SHAKE, P57; GUAVA-GLAZED PORK TENDERLOIN, P96; GUAVA ICE CREAM WITH BLACKBERRY COULIS, P120.

Quinoa

✔ Lifts mood
✔ Aids restful sleep and reduces fatigue
✔ Balances blood-sugar levels
✔ Eases chronic pain
✔ Protects hair and restores color
✔ Reduces age spots and wrinkles
✔ Improves memory and cognition
✔ Encourages healthy digestion
✔ Supports bone health
✔ Reduces inflammation

Quinoa is a nutritious, protein-rich seed full of B vitamins, fiber, and iron that lift energy levels and mood. It contains all of the amino acids needed to create and protect cells, and is rich in antioxidants and omega oils.

It's rich in...

→ Amino acids, to nourish the hair follicles and promote growth; tyrosine can encourage repigmentation of the hair
→ Melatonin, to encourage restful sleep and healthy sleep patterns
→ Lysine, to help your body absorb calcium to protect bones; produces elastin and collagen for healthy skin
→ Fiber, to balance blood-sugar levels, support the liver and healthy digestion, ease constipation, and stabilize mood

Use in... soups, casseroles, stir-fries, and stews; instead of rice or couscous in salads; as a bed for curries, tagines, chili, and roasted vegetable dishes; salad with dried cherries, pistachios, artichoke hearts, lemon juice, olive oil, and parsley; loaves and cakes with dried fruit and nuts; breakfast cereal with almond or soymilk and fresh fruit.

SEE: POACHED EGGS ON QUINOA HASH BROWNS, P49; MEDITERRANEAN STUFFED BELL PEPPERS, P82; ASPARAGUS & PEA QUINOA RISOTTO, P99; TOASTED QUINOA, TUNA & LENTIL SALAD, P98.

Garlic

✔ Helps immunity and digestion
✔ Lifts mood and energy levels
✔ Supports the nervous system
✔ Essential for heart and brain health
✔ Necessary for skin and eye health
✔ Regulates blood-sugar levels
✔ Encourages restful sleep and oral health
✔ Reduces blood pressure and cholesterol

Garlic can prevent cardiovascular disease, arthritis, and cataracts, improve circulation, rejuvenate skin, and increase energy levels. Studies also suggest that it prevents and delays chronic diseases that occur with age.

It's rich in...

→ Vitamin B_6, which encourages healthy iron levels to boost energy and mood and keep the heart and brain functioning optimally; prevents premature gray hair
→ Sulfur, to produce collagen, which fights wrinkles and inflammation, protects from free radicals, and maintains healthy gums
→ Allicin, to promote circulation, which aids skin, heart, memory, and hair growth, and reduces blood pressure and inflammation
→ Selenium and vitamin C, which can help delay and reverse the signs of aging

Use in... salad dressings, stews, dips, soups, and casseroles; roast and spread on whole-grain bread; curries; pasta sauces; aïoli; flavor steamed vegetables; spread on fish; bake with shallots in sherry; rub into the skin of a whole chicken and fill the cavity with garlic cloves; creamy yogurt sauces served with leafy greens, lamb, or poultry.

SEE: VIRTUALLY EVERY SAVORY DIP OR COOKED RECIPE IN THIS BOOK, ESPECIALLY CARAMELIZED GARLIC TART, P106; AÏOLI WITH CRISPBREADS & CRUDITÉS, P54; SPAGHETTI WITH OLIVE OIL, GARLIC & CHILE, P111.

Eggs

- ✔ Regulate mood
- ✔ Encourage concentration and alertness
- ✔ Stabilize blood sugar
- ✔ Promote sleep and relaxation
- ✔ Maintain healthy skin and hair
- ✔ Protect eyesight
- ✔ Support brain and heart health
- ✔ Help prevent bone loss
- ✔ Boost metabolism

One of the most important sources of high-quality protein, eggs contain amino acids, which are essential for the building and repair of body tissues, such as skin and muscles. They provide a great source of sustainable energy, which will help balance weight and beat fatigue. What's more, they are fabulous for heart health and help reverse the symptoms of stress, including easing palpitations.

They are rich in...

- → Betaine and choline, which are both essential for the healthy functioning of the brain, and nervous and cardiovascular systems
- → Vitamin D, to encourage healthy bones and teeth
- → Lutein and zeaxanthin, which are required for healthy eyesight

Use in... omelets with spinach, herbs, and mushrooms; simply boil an egg for an easy, nutritious snack; scramble with chives and top with smoked salmon or other oily fish; chop and add to salads; poach and serve with spinach, asparagus, or broiled portabello mushrooms; use in frittatas with feta cheese and peas, zucchini, and other green vegetables.

SEE: HUEVOS RANCHEROS, P48; BAKED AVOCADO EGG CUPS, P44; POACHED EGGS ON QUINOA HASH BROWNS, P49; BROCCOLI & RED PEPPER FRITTATA, P46; BANANA, OAT & BLACKBERRY MUFFINS, P68; AÏOLI WITH CRISPBREADS & CRUDITÉS, P54; PESTO BROCCOLI WITH POACHED EGGS, P80; FENNEL & MUSHROOM TARTS, P86; CARAMELIZED GARLIC TART, P106; BLACKBERRY BRÛLÉES, P123.

WHAT'S YOUR PROBLEM?

These functional foods contain the nutrients that target specific problems related to the effects of aging, both internal and external. Decide which symptoms affect you and choose from the foods and recipes that can relieve them. These icons are used throughout the recipe section to highlight which recipes can help combat which symptoms.

Wrinkles

Cranberries, guavas, sardines, tomatoes, avocados, broccoli, pomegranates, dark chocolate, carrots, leafy greens, fennel, eggplant, Brazil nuts, red bell peppers, eggs, quinoa, olive oil, garlic, cinnamon, blackberries, oats, watercress, tuna
Recipes include:
Oat crackers, p63; Banana, oat & blackberry muffins, p68; Toasted quinoa, tuna & lentil salad, p98; Guava ice cream with blackberry coulis, p120.

Age spots

Cranberries, olive oil, sardines, dark chocolate, broccoli, avocados, Brazil nuts, tuna, red bell peppers, guavas, eggplant, carrots, pomegranates, quinoa, cinnamon, watercress, fennel
Recipes include:
Spicy Brazil nuts, p56; Fennel & mushroom tarts, p86; Chicken mole, p92; Guava-glazed pork tenderloin, p96.

Dry skin

Sardines, avocados, dark chocolate, red bell peppers, eggs, carrots, olive oil, pomegranates, quinoa, leafy greens, garlic, cranberries, fennel, blackberries, Brazil nuts, eggplant, broccoli, guavas, fennel
Recipes include:
Baked avocado egg cups, p44; Roasted chile & lemon sardines, p84; Broccoli salad with dill & pine nuts, p76; Tuna with bell peppers & fennel gratin, p104.

Tooth decay

Cranberries, dark chocolate, guavas, cinnamon, garlic, watercress, tuna, olive oil, eggs, sardines, broccoli
Recipes include:
On-the-go granola bars, p40; Watercress soup with cheese and oat crackers, p88; Sesame-crusted tuna with ginger dressing, p102; Cranberry ice cream with dark chocolate, p118.

Spider veins

Sardines, tomatoes, pomegranates, dark chocolate, tuna, avocados, oats, eggplant, red bell peppers, eggs, carrots, quinoa, cinnamon, olive oil, garlic, blackberries, broccoli, leafy greens, Brazil nuts, fennel, guavas, watercress

Recipes include:
Guava & ginger smoothie, p38; Citrus olives, p50; Eggplant, chickpea & paneer curry, p110; Pomegranate panna cotta, p122.

Lack of libido

Dark chocolate, carrots, oats, watercress, Brazil nuts, blackberries, cinnamon, garlic

Recipes include:
Berry & coconut porridge, p43; Carrot & beet tabbouleh, p78; Spicy Brazil nuts, p56; Caramelized garlic tart, p106.

Thinning hair

Sardines, avocados, eggplant, red bell peppers, eggs, pomegranates, Brazil nuts, olive oil, carrots, fennel, oats, blackberries, watercress, tuna, broccoli, quinoa, tomatoes, garlic

Recipes include:
Smoky eggplant dip, p53; Carrot, cilantro & lentil soup, p91; Fennel-roasted lamb with figs, p94; Hearty ratatouille, p108.

Gray hair

Quinoa, carrots, dark chocolate, tomatoes, eggs, broccoli, garlic, red bell peppers, Brazil nuts, blackberries, tuna, watercress, sardines

Recipes include:
Broccoli & red pepper frittata, p46; Asparagus & pea quinoa risotto, p99; Butternut, broccoli & mushroom gratin, p105; Apple & blackberry compote with almond scones, p124.

Weak bones

Sardines, broccoli, pomegranates, eggs, blackberries, tuna, watercress, quinoa, olive oil, cinnamon, tomatoes, eggplant
Recipes include: Poached eggs on quinoa hash browns, p49; Bruschetta with tomatoes & basil, p62; Roasted chile & lemon sardines, p84; Guava-glazed pork tenderloin, p96.

Poor circulation

Cranberries, sardines, dark chocolate, carrots, eggplant, red bell peppers, cinnamon, pomegranates, eggs, blackberries, garlic, broccoli
Recipes include: Blueberry pomegranate smoothie, p36; Spiced raisin & cranberry cookies, p64; Eggplant & sesame noodle salad, p70; Blackberry brûlées, p123.

Eyesight

Sardines, avocado, eggplant, red bell peppers, tomatoes, pomegranate, eggs, carrots, guava, fennel, blackberries, tuna, broccoli
Recipes Include: Baked avocado egg cups, p44; Carrot & Puy lentil salad, p75; Avocado & sardine salad with zesty dressing, p72; Guava ice cream with blackberry coulis, p120.

Poor sleep

Dark chocolate, avocados, red bell peppers, eggs, guavas, oats, blackberries, tuna, quinoa, broccoli, cinnamon, garlic
Recipes include: Huevos rancheros, p48; Chilled avocado soup, p90; Butternut, broccoli & mushroom gratin, p105; Bananas with spiced chocolate, p116.

Low energy

Sardines, dark chocolate, avocados, eggplant, red bell peppers, garlic, eggs, Brazil nuts, pomegranates, carrots, guavas, fennel, oats, watercress, tuna, broccoli, quinoa
Recipes include:
Fruit & nut muesli, p42; Aïoli with crispbreads & crudités, p54; Fennel & cumin Waldorf salad, p74; Tuna with bell peppers & fennel gratin, p104.

Joint pain & stiffness

Dark chocolate, olive oil, cranberries, oats, sardines, Brazil nuts, avocados, red bell peppers, tuna, eggs, blackberries, pomegranates, cinnamon, tomatoes,
Recipes include:
Avocado & tomato tostados, p60; Avocado & sardine salad with zesty dressing, p72; Chicken mole, p92; Pomegranate panna cotta, p122.

Poor memory & forgetfulness

Cranberries, olive oil, sardines, dark chocolate, quinoa eggplant, red bell peppers, avocado, pomegranate, eggs, Brazil nuts, oats, blackberries, watercress, tuna, broccoli, cinnamon
Recipes Include:
Berry & Brazil nut smoothie, p39; Cranberry muffins, p69; Toasted quinoa, tuna & lentil salad, p98; Molten chocolate lava cakes, p115.

Cellulite

Cranberries, dark chocolate, red bell peppers, tomatoes, eggplant, fennel, pomegranates, eggs, carrots, guavas, cinnamon, blackberries, garlic, broccoli, quinoa
Recipes include:
Carrot chips with honey yogurt dip, p58; Pesto broccoli with poached eggs, p80; Mediterranean stuffed bell peppers, p82; Baked honey, cardamom & cinnamon figs, p112.

PUTTING IT ALL TOGETHER

Meal Planner	Monday	Tuesday	Wednesday
Breakfast	Fruit & nut muesli, p42	On-the-go granola bars, p40	Berry & coconut oatmeal, p43
Morning snack	Guava & mango shake, p57	Spicy Brazil nuts, p56	Bruschetta with tomatoes & basil, p62
Lunch	Carrot & Puy lentil salad, p75	Eggplant & sesame noodle salad, p70	Pesto broccoli with poached eggs, p80
Afternoon snack	Carrot chips with honey yogurt dip, p58	Aïoli with crispbreads & crudités, p54	Citrus olives, p50
Dinner	Spaghetti with olive oil, garlic & chile, p111	Tuna with bell peppers & fennel gratin, p104	Miso eggplant with rice noodles, p100
Dessert	Blackberry brûlées, p123	Cranberry ice cream with dark chocolate, p118	Baked honey, cardamom & cinnamon figs, p112

Thursday	Friday	Saturday	Sunday
Baked avocado egg cups, p44	Guava & ginger smoothie, p38	Huevos rancheros, p48	Poached eggs on quinoa hash browns, p49
Smoky eggplant dip, p53	Spiced raisin & cranberry cookies, p64	Carrot & lentil muffins, p66	Fresh pomegranate
Gazpacho, p83	Broccoli salad with dill & pine nuts, p76	Mediterranean stuffed bell peppers, p82	Watercress soup with cheese and oat crackers, p88
Cranberry muffins, p69	Avocado & tomato tostados, p60	Greek feta & mint dip, p52	Citrus olives, p50
Toasted quinoa, tuna & lentil salad, p98	Caramelized garlic tart, p106	Guava-glazed pork tenderloin, p96	Chicken mole, p92
Pomegranate panna cotta, p122	Bananas with spiced chocolate, p116	Fruit salsa & cinnamon triangles, p114	Apple & blackberry compote with almond scones, p124

Meal Planner	Monday	Tuesday	Wednesday
Breakfast	Berry & coconut oatmeal, p43	Berry & Brazil nut smoothie, p39	On-the-go granola bars, p40
Morning snack	Spicy Brazil nuts, p56	Spiced raisin & cranberry cookies, p64	A few Brazil nuts covered in dark chocolate
Lunch	Avocado & sardine salad with zesty dressing, p72	Fennel & mushroom tarts, p86	Chilled avocado soup, p90
Afternoon snack	Bruschetta with tomatoes & basil, p62	Carrot chips with honey yogurt dip, p58	Aïoli with crispbreads & crudités, p54
Dinner	Asparagus & pea quinoa risotto, p99	Sesame-crusted tuna with ginger dressing, p102	Hearty ratatouille, p108
Dessert	Guava ice cream with blackberry coulis, p120	Molten chocolate lava cakes, p115	Pomegranate panna cotta, p122

WEEK 2

Thursday	Friday	Saturday	Sunday
Fruit & nut muesli, p42	Blueberry pomegranate smoothie, p36	Broccoli & red pepper frittata, p46	Baked avocado egg cups, p44
Smoky eggplant dip, p53	Avocado & tomato tostados, p60	Carrot & lentil muffins, p66	Spicy Brazil nuts, p56
Fennel & cumin Waldorf salad, p74	Carrot, cilantro & lentil soup, p91	Roasted chile & lemon sardines, p84	Carrot & beet tabbouleh, p78
Carrot & lentil muffins, p66	Rosemary oat crackers, p63	Greek feta & mint dip, p52	Spiced raisin & cranberry cookies, p64
Butternut, broccoli & mushroom gratin, p105	Eggplant, chickpea & paneer curry, p110	Fennel-roasted lamb with figs, p94	Toasted quinoa, tuna & lentil salad, p98
Baked honey, cardamom & cinnamon figs, p112	Fruit salsa & cinnamon triangles, p114	Pomegranate panna cotta, p122	Cranberry ice cream with dark chocolate, p118

YOUNG
RECIPES

BLUEBERRY POMEGRANATE SMOOTHIE

This fresh, fruity smoothie has superior antioxidant levels and is guaranteed to lift your mood and energy levels.

Preparation time: 5 minutes
Serves 4
....

2¾ cups **blueberries**
2½ cups **pomegranate juice**
½ cup **pomegranate seeds**
3½ cups **baby spinach**
2 **bananas**, peeled and cut into chunks
10 **ice cubes**

Put all the ingredients in a blender or food processor and blend until smooth. Serve icy cold in 4 glasses.
....

GUAVA & GINGER SMOOTHIE

Kick-start the day with circulation-boosting ginger and a wealth of antioxidants to protect your cells against the ravages of time.

Preparation time: 10 minutes
Serves 4
....

2 **guavas**, peeled, seeded,
and cut into chunks
½ **pineapple**, peeled, cored,
and cut into chunks
2 **bananas**, peeled and cut into chunks
¾ inch piece of fresh **ginger root**, peeled
and sliced
1¾ cups **almond milk**
10 **ice cubes**

Put all the ingredients in a blender or food processor and blend until smooth and creamy. Serve icy cold.
....

BERRY & BRAZIL NUT SMOOTHIE

Rich in healthy proteins, omega oils, and antioxidants, this fresh, filling smoothie is a pick-me-up that will keep you up!

Preparation time: 10 minutes
Serves 4
....

1⅓ cups fresh or frozen **strawberries**, hulled
1⅓ cups fresh or frozen **raspberries**
1⅓ cups fresh or frozen **blackberries**
¾ cup raw **Brazil nuts**
1 **banana**, peeled and cut into chunks
1 teaspoon **ground cinnamon**
1¼ cups **soymilk**
1 tablespoon **honey**
10 **ice cubes**

Put all the ingredients in a blender or food processor and blend for about 5 minutes until smooth. Serve icy cold.
....

ON-THE-GO GRANOLA BARS

There's no need to make compromises when eating breakfast on the run: these granola bars pack a punch with cinnamon, oats, fruit, nuts, and seeds.

Preparation time: 5 minutes
Cooking time: 20 minutes
Makes 9

6 tablespoons **butter**, plus extra for greasing
¾ cup **honey**
½ teaspoon **ground cinnamon**
¾ cup coarsely chopped **dried apricots**
½ cup coarsely chopped **dried papaya** or **mango**
⅓ cup **raisins**
¼ cup mixed **seeds**, such as **pumpkin**, **sesame**, and **sunflower**
½ cup coarsely chopped **pecans**
1⅔ cups rolled **oats**

Grease a shallow 8-inch square pan.

Put the butter and honey in a saucepan and bring to a boil, stirring constantly, until the mixture bubbles. Add the cinnamon, dried fruit, seeds, and nuts, and then stir and let heat through for 1 minute. Remove the saucepan from the heat and add the oats. Stir well, then transfer to the prepared pan and press down well. Bake in a preheated oven, at 375°F, for 15 minutes or until the top is just beginning to brown.

Let cool in the pan, then cut into 9 squares or bars to serve.

FRUIT & NUT MUESLI

The Brazil nuts in this muesli provide age-defying selenium, the seeds provide omega-3s, and the cranberries will help maintain your teeth and skin. Divine!

Preparation time: 5 minutes
Serves 4

2¼ cups rolled **oats**
⅔ cup **dried cranberries**
⅓ cup chopped **dried apricots**
⅓ cup chopped **dates**
½ cup chopped **pecans**
½ cup chopped **Brazil nuts**
3 to 4 tablespoons **seeds** (**sunflower, pumpkin**, and **sesame**)

To serve
milk
plain yogurt
fresh fruit

Mix all the dry ingredients together.

Divide among 4 bowls and serve with milk, yogurt, and fresh fruit.

BERRY & COCONUT OATMEAL

Bursting with B vitamins, insoluble fiber, and antioxidants, this is the most delicious oatmeal you'll ever taste.

Preparation time: 5 minutes
Cooking time: 10 minutes
Serves 4

2½ cups rolled **oats**
2½ cups **milk**
¼ cup **plain yogurt**
1½ cups fresh **berries**, such as **raspberries**, **blueberries**, and hulled **strawberries**, halved or quartered
3 tablespoons **dried shredded coconut**, plus extra to sprinkle
¼ cup **honey**

Put the rolled oats and coconut shreds into a saucepan with the milk and 2½ cups water. Bring to a boil, then simmer for 8 minutes, or until creamy and thick, stirring often.

Pour into 4 warm bowls and stir in a swirl of the yogurt.

Top with the berries and a drizzle of honey, then sprinkle with a little extra coconut.

BAKED AVOCADO EGG CUPS

Fresh cilantro, crispy bacon, salsa, cheese, or sour cream also make great toppings for this rejuvenating breakfast.

Preparation time: 5 minutes
Cooking time: 15 minutes
Serves 4

2 **avocados**, halved and seeded
4 **eggs**
½ teaspoon **cayenne pepper**
sea salt and **black pepper**
1 tablespoon chopped **chives**, to garnish

Arrange the avocado halves, cut side up, in the holes of a muffin pan or in individual ramekins. Break an egg into each one, sprinkle with the cayenne pepper, and season to taste.

Place in a preheated oven, at 350°F, for about 15 minutes, or until the egg yolks are just set. Garnish with the chives and serve hot.

BROCCOLI & RED PEPPER FRITTATA

This tasty frittata makes a wonderful, nutritious breakfast for a lazy morning, but it could also be enjoyed warm or cold with salad for a light lunch.

Preparation time: 10 minutes
Cooking time: 15 minutes
Serves 4

6 **eggs**
2 tablespoons **milk**
sea salt and **black pepper**
3½ oz sharp **cheddar cheese**, shredded, divided
1 head of **broccoli**, cut into florets
1 tablespoon **olive oil**
1 **red bell pepper**, cored, seeded, and thinly sliced
1 **leek**, white part only, thinly sliced
⅔ cup quartered **cherry tomatoes**

Put the eggs and milk in a mixing bowl and beat until fluffy. Season to taste, add half the shredded cheese, and mix well. Set to one side.

Cook the broccoli florets in a saucepan of lightly salted boiling water for 1 minute, then refresh in cold water and drain well.

Heat the oil in a large, nonstick ovenproof skillet over medium heat and add the bell pepper and leek. Cook for about 2 minutes, or until the leek starts to soften. Then add the broccoli and cherry tomatoes.

Cook for another 2 to 3 minutes, season to taste, and then arrange the vegetables evenly over the bottom of the skillet. Pour in the egg mixture and continue cooking for about 3 minutes, or until the egg sets around the edges.

Place the skillet under a preheated medium-hot broiler for about 5 minutes or until the frittata is golden and set. Sprinkle with the remaining cheddar and return to the broiler until the cheese bubbles. Transfer the to a plate and serve in wedges.

HUEVOS RANCHEROS

Full of rejuvenating garlic, red bell peppers, and tomatoes, this Mexican classic is the perfect dish for a weekend breakfast that everyone in the family will want to share.

Preparation time: 10 minutes
Cooking time: 10 minutes
Serves 4

2 tablespoons **olive oil**
1 large **onion**, diced
2 **red bell peppers**, seeded and diced
2 **garlic cloves**, crushed
¾ teaspoon dried **oregano**
1 (14½ oz) can diced **tomatoes**
4 **eggs**
2 tablespoons crumbled **feta cheese**
4 pieces of **gluten-free pita bread**, toasted, to serve

Heat the oil in a skillet over medium heat. Add the onion, bell peppers, garlic, and oregano and cook for 5 minutes.

Add the tomatoes and cook for another 5 minutes. Pour the tomato mixture into a shallow baking dish and make 4 dips in the mixture.

Crack the eggs into the dips, scatter with the feta, and cook under a preheated hot broiler for 3 to 4 minutes.

Serve with the toasted pita bread.

POACHED EGGS ON QUINOA HASH BROWNS

Full of protein and omega-3s, this tasty breakfast is packed with nutrients to keep you looking and feeling young.

Preparation time: 15 minutes, plus chilling
Cooking time: 30 minutes
Serves 4
....

1 teaspoon **vinegar**
4 large **eggs**
sea salt and **black pepper**
2 **scallions**, minced, to garnish

Hash browns
⅔ cup **quinoa**
6 large **potatoes**, peeled and grated
1 **egg**, lightly beaten
1 teaspoon **ground cumin**
2 tablespoons **olive oil**

Cook the quinoa in a saucepan of lightly salted boiling water or according to the package instructions until tender. Refresh in cold water and drain well.

Put the grated potato on a clean dish towel, wrap tightly, and squeeze out the excess moisture. Transfer to a mixing bowl and add the egg, quinoa, and cumin. Season to taste and stir to combine well. Shape the mixture into 8 patties with your hands, arrange on a plate, and chill it in the refrigerator for 15 minutes or overnight.

Heat the oil in a large skillet over medium heat. Cook the patties in 2 batches for about 8 minutes each side, or until crisp, golden, and cooked through. Drain on paper towels.

Meanwhile, bring a saucepan of water to the boil and add the vinegar. Reduce the heat to a very low simmer. Then break the eggs gently into the water. Cook for 5 minutes or until the whites are cooked through and the yolks are still runny.

Divide the hash browns among 4 plates and top with the poached eggs. Season to taste and sprinkle with the scallions to serve.

CITRUS OLIVES

A sunny snack with all the heart-healthy goodness of olive oil and the zing of fennel seeds, with an added citrus twist.

Preparation time: 5 minutes, plus marinating (optional)
Cooking time: 1 minutes
Serves 6

2 teaspoons **fennel seeds**
finely grated zest and juice of ½ **lemon**
finely grated zest and juice of ¼ **orange**
⅓ cup **olive oil**
4 cups mixed **olives**

Add the fennel seeds to a small, dry skillet over medium heat and toast for 30 seconds, or until they start to pop and emit an aroma. Remove from the pan and coarsely crush.

Mix together the fennel seeds, lemon and orange zests and juices, and olive oil in a nonmetallic bowl, and then stir in the olives. Either serve immediately, or cover and let marinate overnight in a cool place.

GREEK FETA & MINT DIP

A light and unbelievably tasty dip, this can also be served with wholewheat pitas, carrot sticks, or broccoli florets.

Preparation time: 5 minutes
Serves 4
·················

1 cup crumbled **feta cheese**
½ small **red onion**, thinly sliced
handful of **mint leaves**, finely chopped
1 cup **Greek yogurt**
freshly ground **black pepper**
sliced ripe **black olives**, to garnish
8 pieces of **whole-wheat pita bread**,
to serve

Mix the cheese with the onion, mint, and yogurt, season with black pepper, and stir gently to combine. Transfer to a serving bowl and sprinkle with a few sliced olives.
···

SMOKY EGGPLANT DIP

This delicious dip is rich in energy-boosting nutrients and will keep your skin and hair looking great.

Preparation time: 20 minutes
Cooking time: 20 minutes
Serves 4 to 6

....

2 large **eggplant**
½ cup **live natural yogurt**
1 **garlic clove**, chopped
1 small **red chile**, seeded and finely chopped
1 teaspoon **ground coriander**
½ teaspoon **ground cumin**
sea salt and **black pepper**
olive oil, to garnish
crudités or **whole-wheat pita bread**, to serve

Place the whole eggplant on a baking sheet, prick all over with a skewer and cook in a preheated oven, at 450°F, for 20 minutes, or until the skins begin to blacken and the eggplant are soft all the way through.

....

Cut the eggplant in half and scrape the soft flesh into the bowl of a food processor. Add the yogurt, garlic clove, chile, coriander, and cumin. Blend until smooth and combined, and then season to taste. Transfer to a bowl and swirl a little olive oil over the top before serving with crudités or pita bread.

....

AÏOLI WITH CRISPBREADS & CRUDITÉS

This intensely garlicky dip is great for the circulation, heart, memory, skin, bones, and hair. It boosts energy levels and eradicates cellulite.

Preparation time: 10 minutes
Serves 4

3 **egg yolks**
5 **garlic cloves**, peeled and coarsely chopped
finely grated zest and juice of 1 **lemon**
1 teaspoon **mustard powder**
sea salt and **black pepper**
⅔ cup **olive oil**

To serve
crispbread
crudités

Put the egg yolks, garlic cloves, lemon zest and juice, and mustard powder in the bowl of a food processer, season to taste, and blend until smooth and frothy.

With the motor still running, add the olive oil in a very slow but steady stream until the mixture becomes thick and unguent. Spoon into a bowl and serve with crispbread and crudités for dipping.

SPICY BRAZIL NUTS

Just a handful of these delicious nuts will boost energy levels and provide valuable omega oils to keep your skin and hair looking their best.

Preparation time: 5 minutes
Cooking time: 10 minutes
Serves 4 to 6

2¼ cups raw **Brazil nuts**
1 tablespoon **rosemary** leaves, finely chopped
1 teaspoon **dark brown sugar**
1 teaspoon **sea salt**
1 teaspoon freshly ground **black pepper**
½ teaspoon **cayenne pepper**
2 tablespoons **olive oil**

Arrange the Brazil nuts on a baking pan and place in a preheated oven, at 350°F, for 10 minutes, or until lightly browned and fragrant.

Meanwhile, put the rosemary, sugar, salt, black pepper, cayenne pepper, and olive oil in a large bowl and mix well.

Add the hot nuts to the flavored oil, stir to coat, and serve warm or cold.

Leftover nuts can be stored in an airtight container for up to a week.

GUAVA & MANGO SHAKE

Bursting with fiber, antioxidants, and protein, this will steady blood-sugar levels and rejuvenate your mind and body.

Preparation time: 10 minutes
Serves 4
....

2 **guavas**, peeled, seeded, and cut into chunks
2 **mangos**, peeled, seeded, and cut into chunks
2 tablespoons **coconut cream**
finely grated zest and juice of 1 **lemon**
2 tablespoons **honey**
2½ cups **skim milk** or **soymilk**
10 **ice cubes**

Put all the ingredients in a blender or food processor and blitz until smooth. Serve the shakes icy cold.
....

CARROT CHIPS WITH HONEY YOGURT DIP

These cinnamon carrot chips are bursting with antioxidants and vitamin A to improve overall health, appearance, and well-being.

Preparation time: 10 minutes, plus cooling
Cooking time: 10 minutes
Serves 4

....

4 large **carrots**
1 tablespoon **olive oil**, plus extra to serve
1 teaspoon **ground cinnamon**
½ teaspoon **ground ginger**
½ teaspoon grated **nutmeg**
pinch of **sea salt**
pinch of **black pepper**
⅔ cup **plain Greek yogurt**
1 tablespoon **honey**

Scrub the carrots then cut them into long, thin strips using a vegetable peeler or sharp knife. The thickness doesn't matter, as long as they are all of a similar size.

....

Mix the olive oil, cinnamon, ginger, nutmeg, salt, and pepper in a large mixing bowl. Add the carrot strips and toss with your hands to coat evenly. Spread the strips out in a single layer on several cookie sheets and place in a preheated oven, at 425°F, for 10 minutes, or until beginning to crisp. Set aside to cool.

....

Meanwhile, mix the yogurt and honey in a small bowl and drizzle with a swirl of olive oil. Serve with the carrots chips.

....

AVOCADO & TOMATO TOSTADOS

With lycopene, powerful antioxidants, and omega-3s, this snack is perfect for beating wrinkles and gray hair.

Preparation time: 15 minutes
Cooking time: 2 minutes
Serves 4

....

4 **corn tortillas**
1 tablespoon **vegetable oil**
2 **avocados**, peeled and seeded
¼ cup **crème fraîche** or **sour cream**
2 to 3 tablespoons **lime juice**
1 tablespoon minced **red onion**
4 **tomatoes**, diced
1 tablespoon extra virgin **olive oil**
salt and **black pepper**
handful of fresh **cilantro**, chopped, plus extra to serve (optional)

Stamp out circles from the tortillas using a 2-inch cookie cutter; alternatively, cut them into wedges. Brush them with vegetable oil, arrange on a baking sheet, and place under a preheated hot broiler. Cook for 1 minute on each side, or until crisp. Remove from the broiler and let cool.

....

Meanwhile, put the avocado flesh and crème fraîche in a food processor and blend until smooth. Stir in 1 tablespoon of the lime juice and season to taste. Stir together the onion, tomatoes, and olive oil in a bowl, add lime juice and season to taste, and stir through the cilantro. Spoon a little of the avocado mixture onto each tortilla circle, and place a teaspoonful of the tomato salsa on top. Sprinkle with more cilantro to serve, if using.

....

BRUSCHETTA WITH TOMATOES & BASIL

Use fresh, firm tomatoes to ensure the highest antioxidant content and prepare yourself for a rejuvenating lycopene hit.

Preparation time: 10 minutes
Cooking time: 5 minutes
Serves 4
....

1⅓ cups quartered **cherry tomatoes**
1 small **red onion**, thinly sliced
1 **garlic clove**, crushed
1 tablespoon **balsamic vinegar**
3 tablespoons **olive oil,** divided
sea salt and **black pepper**
4 thick slices of **brown sourdough bread**
handful of **basil** leaves, torn

Put the tomatoes in a bowl with the onion, garlic, vinegar, and half the olive oil. Season to taste, stir to combine, and set aside.
....

Brush both sides of the bread slices with the remaining oil and place under a preheated hot broiler until browned all over. Transfer to a plate and top with the tomato mixture, juice and all, and sprinkle with the basil. Season with freshly ground black pepper to serve.
....

ROSEMARY OAT CRACKERS

These oaty crackers are simply delicious on their own or topped with cream cheese and a few purple-red grapes.

Preparation time: 15 minutes
Cooking time: 15 minutes
Makes 20 to 24

....

2 cups rolled **oats**
3 **rosemary** sprigs, leaves stripped
1 cup **all-purpose flour**, plus extra for dusting
¾ teaspoon **baking powder**
pinch of **salt**
6 tablespoons chilled unsalted **butter**, diced
½ cup **milk**

Put the rolled oats and rosemary in a food processor and blend just until they resemble bread crumbs. Add the flour, baking powder, and salt and process again. Add the butter, then process until it is mixed in. With the motor still running, pour in the milk through the feed tube until the dough forms a ball.

....

Turn the dough out onto a floured surface and roll out to about ¼ inch thick. Cut out 20 to 24 circles, using a 2 to 2½-inch plain round cookie cutter, rerolling the leftover dough as necessary.

....

Arrange all the crackers on a cookie sheet and bake in a preheated oven, at 375°F, for 12 to 15 minutes or until golden at the edges. Transfer to a wire rack. Once cool, store in an airtight container.

....

SPICED RAISIN & CRANBERRY COOKIES

Jewel-like cranberries are excellent for your heart, brain, kidneys, digestive system, skin, and teeth, so these are the perfect guilt-free snack.

Preparation time: 10 minutes
Cooking time: 15 minutes
Makes 8

1 stick (½ cup) **butter**
⅔ cup firmly packed light **brown sugar**
1 tablespoon light **corn syrup**
1 cup **all-purpose flour**
1 teaspoon **baking powder**
½ teaspoon ground **allspice**
1⅓ cups rolled **oats**
⅓ cup **raisins**
⅓ cup dried **cranberries**

Use nonstick parchment paper to line 2 cookie sheets.

Heat the butter, sugar, and corn syrup in a saucepan over medium heat and stir until just melted. Remove from the heat and add the flour, baking powder, allspice, oats, and fruit. Stir to combine.

Roll the mixture into 8 balls, place them on the lined cookie sheets, and flatten slightly. Bake the cookies in a preheated oven, at 350°F, for 10 to 12 minutes or until golden.

CARROT & LENTIL MUFFINS

High in fiber and full of carroty goodness, these yummy muffins are so irresistible you'll never manage to stop at one.

Preparation time: 10 minutes
Cooking time: 30 minutes
Makes 12

⅓ cup **red lentils**
2¼ cups **plain wholemeal flour**
2 tablespoons **ground flax seed**
1½ teaspoons **baking powder**
¼ cup firmly packed light **brown sugar**
1 teaspoon ground **cinnamon**
½ teaspoon ground **cloves**
3 tablespoons **applesauce**
3 tablespoons **honey**
3 tablespoons **sunflower oil**
1 **egg**
1 large **carrot**, peeled and coarsely grated
2 to 3 tablespoons **soymilk** (optional)

Line the cups of a 12-cup muffin pan with paper muffin cups.

Cook the red lentils in 1¼ cups water for 8 minutes, or until soft. Drain in a sieve.

Sift the flour, flax seed, and baking powder into a large bowl, and then stir in the sugar and spices.

Put the lentils into a food processor with the applesauce, honey, sunflower oil, and egg and blend until smooth.

Pour the wet ingredients into the dry ones, stirring in the grated carrots when nearly blended. Add some soymilk to loosen the batter, if needed.

Spoon the batter into the muffin cups and bake them in a preheated oven, at 350°F, for 18 to 20 minutes or until they are risen and golden. Transfer to a rack to cool.

BANANA, OAT & BLACKBERRY MUFFINS

These muffins have plenty of fiber and a host of antioxidants and omega oils to encourage well-being on all levels.

Preparation time: 15 minutes
Cooking time: 20 minutes
Makes 12

2½ cups **all-purpose flour**
3½ teaspoons **baking soda**
⅔ cup **dark brown sugar**
½ cup **steel-cut oats**
2 ripe **bananas**, peeled
1 cup **live plain yogurt**
⅓ cup **olive oil**
2 **eggs**, lightly beaten
1 cup **blackberries**
1 teaspoon **ground cinnamon**
1 teaspoon **demerara sugar**

Line the cups of a 12-cup muffin pan with paper muffin cups.

Sift the flour, baking soda, and dark brown sugar into a large bowl and stir in the oats. Mash together the bananas, yogurt, oil, and eggs in a separate bowl and stir until well blended and fairly smooth.

Fold the banana mixture into the flour bowl and gently stir with a metal spoon until only just combined. The resulting mixture should look craggy, with specks of flour still visible. Fold in the blackberries so that they are mixed in but not crushed.

Divide the batter among the muffin cups. Combine the cinnamon and demerara sugar and sprinkle the mixture onto the muffins.

Place the muffins in a preheated oven, at 350°F, for 20 minutes or until golden and well risen. Serve warm or cold. The muffins can be stored in an airtight container for up to4 days and can be frozen.

CRANBERRY MUFFINS

Light and fluffy, these scrumptious muffins contain antioxidant-rich cranberries and flavonoid-rich chocolate.

Preparation time: 10 minutes
Cooking time: 20 minutes
Makes 12

2⅓ cups **all-purpose flour**
4 teaspoons **baking powder**
⅓ cup firmly packed light **brown sugar**
3 pieces of **preserved ginger** from a jar, finely chopped (about ¼ cup)
⅔ cup **dried cranberries**
⅔ cup **dark chocolate chips**
1 **egg**
1 cup **skim milk**
¼ cup **vegetable oil**

Line the cups of a 12-cup muffin pan with paper muffin cups.

Sift the flour and baking powder into a large bowl. Add the sugar, ginger, cranberries, and chocolate chips and stir to combine.

In a separate bowl, beat together the egg, milk, and oil, and then add the wet mixture to the flour mixture. Using a large metal spoon, gently stir the liquid into the flour until just combined. The batter should look craggy, with specks of flour still visible.

Divide the batter among the muffin cups, piling it up in the center. Bake in a preheated oven, at 400°F, for 18 to 20 minutes or until well risen and golden. Transfer to a wire rack to cool, but serve while still slightly warm.

EGGPLANT & SESAME NOODLE SALAD

This Chinese-inspired salad is delicious both hot or cold, so it is ideal for lunchboxes, and it comes with the rejuvenating power of eggplant to boot!

Preparation time: 25 minutes
Cooking time: 30 minutes
Serves 4

....

2 **eggplant**
1 teaspoon **chili oil**
¼ cup **sesame oil**
3 tablespoons **honey**
¼ cup **sweet chili sauce**
⅓ cup light **soy sauce**
2 tablespoons **Chinese rice wine**
3 tablespoons **sesame seeds**, toasted
6 oz dried **fine egg noodles**
1 teaspoon peeled and finely chopped fresh **ginger root**
1 **garlic clove**, crushed
1 cup **baby spinach**
1 **red bell pepper**, seeded and finely chopped
8 **scallions**, thinly sliced
½ cup **bean sprouts**
large handful of coarsely chopped **cilantro leaves**

Prick each eggplant all over with a skewer, put it onto a cookie sheet, and bake in a preheated oven, at 400°F, for 30 minutes or until softened. Let cool.

Meanwhile, combine the oils, honey, sweet chili sauce, soy sauce, and rice wine, in a bowl. Stir in the sesame seeds and divide the dressing between 2 wide bowls.

Cook the noodles in a saucepan of boiling water for about 3 minutes or according to the package directions, until just tender. Drain, add to one of the bowls of dressing, and toss to coat evenly.

Mix the ginger and garlic into the remaining bowl of dressing.

Cut the eggplant in half lengthwise and peel away and discard the skin. Use a spoon to scoop the flesh into the dressing bowl. Stir in the spinach, red bell pepper, scallions, and bean sprouts, then add the dressed noodles and toss to mix well. Sprinkle the salad with the cilantro leaves to serve.

AVOCADO & SARDINE SALAD WITH ZESTY DRESSING

This tangy, fragrant salad offers a burst of protein, omega-3 oils, healthy fats, and vitamin E to stop aging in its tracks.

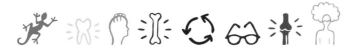

Preparation time: 15 minutes
Serves 4

2 (4 oz) cans **sardines** in olive oil, drained and chopped
handful of fresh **cilantro**, finely chopped, plus extra to serve
1 **celery** stalk, finely chopped
1 **scallion**, finely chopped
2 tablespoons good-quality **mayonnaise**
finely grated zest and juice of 1 **lime**
sea salt and **black pepper**
3 handfuls of mixed **salad greens**
2 **avocados**, peeled, seeded, and cut into wedges

Dressing
finely grated zest and juice of 1 **lime**
2 tablespoons **extra virgin olive oil**
½ teaspoon **sea salt**
½ teaspoon **sugar**
2 tablespoons finely chopped fresh **cilantro**
1 tablespoon **coconut cream**

Put the sardines, cilantro, celery, scallion, mayonnaise, and lime zest and juice in a large bowl, season to taste, and toss well together. Whisk together the dressing ingredients in a separate bowl.

Arrange the salad greens on a large plate and sprinkle the avocado wedges on top. Place the sardine mixture in a mound in the center and drizzle the dressing evenly over everything. Scatter with a few extra cilantro leaves and give it a good grating of black pepper. Serve immediately.

FENNEL & CUMIN WALDORF SALAD

A new twist on the world-famous salad created at New York's Waldorf Hotel, this one benefits from all the super-nutrients of fabulous fennel.

Preparation time: 10 minutes
Cooking time: 5 minutes
Serves 4

½ cup **walnut** pieces
1 teaspoon **ground cumin**
1¼ cups **live plain yogurt**
⅔ cup halved **green grapes**
1 small **fennel bulb**, thinly sliced
6 **celery stalks**, sliced diagonally
1 **green apple**, cored, quartered, and thinly sliced
½ cup **golden raisins**

Heat a nonstick skillet over medium-low heat and dry-fry the walnut pieces for 3 to 4 minutes, stirring frequently, until slightly golden. Remove from the heat and let cool slightly.

Mix together the cumin and yogurt in a large bowl. Add the remaining ingredients and the toasted walnuts and toss in the dressing until well coated.

Serve the salad immediately or cover and chill until required.

CARROT & PUY LENTIL SALAD

With plenty of antioxidants, protein, B vitamins, and fiber, this surprisingly sweet salad is a great choice to form the mainstay of any anti-aging diet!

Preparation time: 15 minutes, plus cooling
Cooking time: 35 minutes
Serves 4

1 lb **carrots**, scrubbed
1 tablespoon **olive oil**
1 tablespoon **cumin seeds**
1 teaspoon **dried thyme**
1 tablespoon clear **honey**
1 (14 oz) can **Puy lentils**, rinsed and drained
1 large **red onion**, diced
¼ cup **apple cider vinegar**
1 tablespoon **hazelnut oil**
sea salt and **black pepper**
large handful of **mint** leaves, chopped
3½ oz **arugula** or **watercress**
3 tablespoons **hazelnuts**, toasted
3½ oz **feta cheese**

Cut the carrots into matchsticks and add to a roasting pan along with the olive oil, cumin, and thyme and toss together to coat. Place in a preheated oven, at 350°F, for 30 minutes, turning frequently. Drizzle with the honey and return to the oven for another 5 minutes. Remove from the oven and let cool.

Meanwhile, put the lentils, onion, vinegar, and hazelnut oil in a large saucepan, season to taste, and heat through gently, stirring frequently. Remove from the heat. When the mixture has cooled, stir in the mint.

To serve, arrange the arugula or watercress on a large plate, top with the lentils, and then the carrots. Sprinkle with the toasted hazelnuts and then crumble the feta cheese evenly over everything. Grind some black pepper over the top and serve.

BROCCOLI SALAD WITH DILL & PINE NUTS

This hearty raw broccoli and fruit salad provides loads of fiber and antioxidants to help turn back the clock.

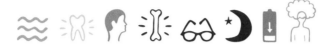

Preparation time: 15 minutes, plus standing
Serves 4
....

2 large heads of **broccoli**,
cut into tiny florets
handful of **watercress**, torn
1 **red onion**, finely sliced
1 cup quartered **grapes**
⅔ cup **blackberries**, halved
¾ cup **dried cranberries**, halved
2½ tablespoons **pomegranate seeds**
⅓ cup **pine nuts**, toasted

Dressing
2 tablespoons good-quality **mayonnaise**
2 tablespoons **live plain yogurt**
finely grated zest and juice of 1 **lemon**
2 tablespoons finely chopped **dill**
sea salt and **black pepper**

Put the broccoli, watercress, onion, grapes, pine nuts, pomegranate seeds, blackberries, and cranberries in a large bowl and toss everything together.

....

Put the dressing ingredients in a small bowl, season to taste, and whisk to combine. Pour it evenly over the salad and toss gently to coat. Let stand for about 10 minutes before serving to allow the flavors to mingle.

....

Leftover salad can be stored in an airtight container in the refrigerator for 2 to 3 days.

....

CARROT & BEET TABBOULEH

With its wide range of age-defying nutrients, this delicious Middle Eastern salad is designed to enhance youthfulness.

Preparation time: 20 minutes
Cooking time: 20 minutes
Serves 4

1 cup **bulgur wheat**
1 **garlic clove**, crushed
pinch of **ground cinnamon**
pinch of **allspice**
2 tablespoons **pomegranate molasses** or **pomegranate juice**
⅓ cup extra virgin **olive oil**
1 **carrot**, grated
2 cooked **beets**, cubed
2 **scallions**, sliced
½ **green chile**, chopped
large handful of **mint**, chopped
large handful of **parsley**, chopped
⅓ cup crumbled **feta cheese**
salt and **black pepper**

Prepare the bulgur wheat according to the package directions, then drain thoroughly.

Combine the garlic, spices, pomegranate molasses, and olive oil in a large bowl. Add the bulgur wheat, carrot, beets, scallions, chile, mint, and parsley, toss gently to coat, and then season to taste. Scatter with the feta to serve.

PESTO BROCCOLI WITH POACHED EGGS

This sensational lunch dish ticks all the boxes when it comes to anti-aging vitamins and minerals, and it's satisfyingly tasty.

Preparation time: 10 minutes
Cooking time: 10 minutes
Serves 4

1¾ lb **broccoli**, chopped into large florets
¾ lb **sugar snap peas**
4 **eggs**
1 cup chopped **sundried tomatoes**
freshly ground **black pepper**
Parmesan cheese shavings,
to serve

Pesto
⅓ cup **basil** leaves
½ tablespoon toasted **pine nuts**
1 tablespoon grated **Parmesan cheese**
1 small **garlic clove**, crushed
3 to 4 teaspoons **olive oil**

To make the pesto, put the basil and pine nuts in a food processor and blend until broken down. Add the cheese and garlic and process briefly. With the motor still running, slowly pour in the oil through the feed tube until combined.

Cook the broccoli and sugar snap peas in a large saucepan of boiling water for 7 to 8 minutes or until "al dente."

Meanwhile, bring a saucepan of water to a gentle simmer and stir it with a large spoon to create a swirl. Break 2 of the eggs into the water and cook for 3 minutes. Remove with a slotted spoon and keep warm. Repeat with the remaining eggs.

Drain the vegetables, then return them to the pan. Add 1½ tablespoons of the pesto (store any remaining pesto in an airtight container in the refrigerator) and the sun-dried tomatoes. Gently toss together until well coated.

Divide the salad among 4 serving plates and set a poached egg on top of each portion. Sprinkle with a few Parmesan shavings, grind over some black pepper, and serve immediately.

MEDITERRANEAN STUFFED BELL PEPPERS

These easy-to-prepare stuffed bell peppers are packed with protein, antioxidants, amino acids, calcium, and omega oils.

Preparation time: 15 minutes
Cooking time: 40 minutes
Serves 4

½ cup **quinoa**
12 **sundried tomatoes in oil**, sliced, plus 2 tablespoons oil from the jar
1 small **onion**, minced
2 **garlic cloves**, crushed
1 teaspoon **dried oregano**
1 teaspoon **dried thyme**
1 tablespoon **balsamic vinegar**
12 **black olives**, sliced
3½ oz **feta cheese**, cubed
handful of **basil** leaves, torn
4 large **red bell peppers**
sea salt and **black pepper**
green salad, to serve

In a large saucepan of lightly salted boiling water, cook the quinoa according to the package instructions, until tender.

Meanwhile, heat the sundried tomato oil in a large saucepan or wok over medium heat, and add the onion, garlic cloves, oregano, and thyme. Cook for 5 to 10 minutes, or until the onion is soft.

Stir in the quinoa, balsamic vinegar, sundried tomatoes, and olives, and cook for another 2 to 3 minutes. Remove the saucepan from the heat, season to taste, and stir in the feta and basil.

Slice the tops off the peppers, retaining the lids, and remove the cores and seeds. Spoon the quinoa mixture into the peppers, replace the lids, and arrange them in a baking dish, standing upright. Cook in a preheated oven, at 350°F, for 20 to 25 minutes, or until the peppers have softened but still have a little bite. Serve the peppers hot or cold with a green salad.

GAZPACHO

The tasty garnish makes this superfood-rich Spanish soup into a fabulous meal in a bowl.

Preparation time: 15 minutes
Cooking time: 5 minutes
Serves 4

4 **red bell peppers**, cored, seeded, and coarsely chopped
1 **red onion**, coarsely chopped
2 **cucumbers**, coarsely chopped
handful of **basil** leaves
handful of **parsley** leaves
2 **garlic cloves**
2 tablespoons **sherry vinegar** or **balsamic vinegar**
⅔ cup **olive oil**
2 cups chilled **tomato juice**
salt and **black pepper**

To serve
1 **avocado**, peeled, stone removed, and chopped
1 soft-cooked **egg**, quartered

Put the vegetables, herbs, and garlic cloves in a food processor and process until the ingredients are finely chopped.

Add the remaining ingredients, season to taste, and process again briefly. Cover and let chill in the fridge for 5 minutes.

Serve in bowls topped with the chopped avocados and quartered eggs.

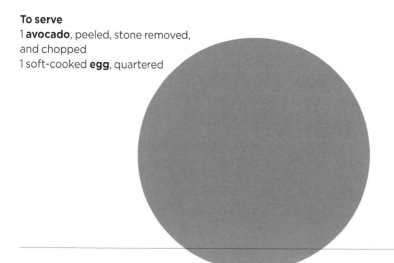

ROASTED CHILE & LEMON SARDINES

An intense lemon flavor, a kick of chile, and all the omega goodness of sardines make this pure youth food on a plate.

Preparation time: 10 minutes
Cooking time: 15 minutes
Serves 4

3 **garlic cloves**, finely sliced
2 **red chiles**, seeded and finely sliced
1 **preserved lemon**, finely sliced
3 tablespoons **olive** or **argan oil**
juice of 1 **lemon**
salt and **black pepper**
8 **sardines**, gutted and cleaned
small bunch of **flat-leaf parsley**, leaves finely chopped, to garnish
chunks of **French bread**, to serve (optional)

Mix together the garlic cloves, chiles, and sliced preserved lemon in a bowl. Then stir in the oil and lemon juice to combine and season well.

Spread some of the mixture on the bottom of a baking dish. Put the sardines on top and spoon the remaining mixture onto the fish. Put into a preheated oven, at 400°F, for 10 to 15 minutes or until the fish is cooked.

Transfer to a serving dish, spoon the cooking juices over the sardines, and garnish with the parsley. Serve with crusty bread, if using.

FENNEL & MUSHROOM TARTS

These luxurious little tarts are packed with protein, fiber, and a wealth of vitamins and minerals to give you a healthy glow.

Preparation time: 15 minutes
Cooking time: 40 minutes
Serves 4

8 oz **ready-made shortcrust pastry flour**, for dusting
3 oz grated **Parmesan cheese,** divided
1 tablespoon **olive oil**
3 **garlic cloves**, crushed
1 small **red onion**, minced
1 teaspoon **dried thyme**
6 oz mixed **mushrooms**
1 **fennel bulb**, thinly sliced
3 **eggs**, lightly beaten
2 oz **Emmental Swiss cheese**
handful of **parsley**, chopped
sea salt and **black pepper**
leafy **green salad**, to serve

Roll out the ready-made pastry on a lightly floured surface to about ⅛ inch thick, and use it to line 4 greased 4-inch tart pans. Rub one-third of the Parmesan gently into the shortcrust pastry lining the pans and let chill in the refrigerator for about 10 minutes.

Heat the oil in a large skillet over medium heat and add the garlic, onion, and thyme. Cook for 5 minutes, or until starting to soften. Add the mushrooms and fennel, cook for another 5 minutes, and then remove from the heat.

Put the eggs in a bowl with the Emmental, the remaining Parmesan, and the parsley. Season to taste and beat together.

Use a slotted spoon to divide the mushroom and fennel mixture among the chilled pastry shells and set them on a cookie sheet. Pour the egg mixture in next, and then place in a preheated oven, at 350°F, for 30 minutes, or until the egg mixture has set. Serve warm or cold with a leafy green salad.

WATERCRESS SOUP WITH CHEESE AND OAT CRACKERS

This calcium- and antioxidant-rich soup can be served hot or cold. The cheese and oat crackers will help steady blood-sugar levels.

Preparation time: 30 minutes
Cooking time: 30 minutes
Serves 4
....

1 tablespoon **olive oil**
3 large **potatoes,**
peeled and cut into chunks
2 **onions,** chopped
1 **garlic clove,** chopped
2½ cups **vegetable** or **chicken stock**
4 large bunches of **watercress,** rinsed and chopped, plus extra, to garnish
finely grated zest and juice of 1 **lemon**
sea salt and **black pepper**
3 tablespoons **Greek yogurt,** to serve

Cheese and oat crackers
1 cup **steel-cut oats**
1½ cups **porridge oats**
3 oz **sharp Cheddar cheese,** grated
¼ cup **olive oil**
⅓ cup plus 1 tablespoon hot **water**
flour, for dusting

Put the oats in a bowl and season. Stir in the cheddar and then the olive oil. Slowly add the hot water, using a fork to combine, until you have a firm dough. Turn out onto an oiled surface and knead until well combined. If the dough is too dry, add more water.
....

Roll out the dough on a lightly floured surface to about ⅛ inch thick. Cut into squares with a knife or cut out shapes with a cookie cutter. Transfer to 2 cookie sheets that are lined with nonstick parchment paper and place in a preheated oven, at 350°F, for 20 minutes. Turn the crackers over and bake for another 10 minutes. Let cool.
....

Meanwhile, heat the oil in a large saucepan over medium heat and add the potatoes, onions, and garlic clove. Cook for 5 minutes, stirring constantly, or until the onions have softened. Add the stock and bring to a boil. Reduce the heat and let simmer for about 20 minutes or until the potatoes are soft.
....

Stir in the watercress and lemon zest and juice and season to taste. Cook for another 2 to 3 minutes, then remove from the heat. Blend until smooth. Top each portion with a swirl of Greek yogurt, a sprig of watercress, and a grating of black pepper. Serve with the crackers on the side.
....

CHILLED AVOCADO SOUP

A sophisticated soup full of omega-3s and anti-aging vitamins A, C, E, and K, as well as heart-healthy potassium.

Preparation time: 10 minutes
Serves 4

3 ripe **avocados**, peeled, seeded, and diced
1 small **red onion**, coarsely chopped
3 to 4 drops **Tabasco sauce**
3 tablespoons **lime juice**
2½ cups **buttermilk**
¼ cup chopped **fresh cilantro**
12 **ice cubes**
soft flour **tortillas**, warmed and cut into strips, to serve

Put the diced avocado in a food processor, reserving a handful for garnish, with all the remaining ingredients, except the ice cubes, and blend until smooth.

Divide among 4 glass bowls and top each portion with 3 ice cubes and some of the reserved avocado. Serve immediately with warmed tortilla strips

CARROT, CILANTRO & LENTIL SOUP

Hormone-balancing carrots combine with high-fiber lentils and fragrant cilantro to make this rich, filling soup.

Preparation time: 10 minutes
Cooking time: 30 minutes
Serves 4

....

2 tablespoons **ghee** or **argan oil**
1 **onion**, minced
¼ cup peeled, chopped **ginger root**
2 to 3 **garlic cloves**, minced
2 teaspoons **coriander seeds**
1 teaspoon **cumin seeds**
1 teaspoon **sugar**
4 **carrots**, peeled and diced
¾ cup **brown lentils**, rinsed
1 to 2 teaspoons **ras el hanout**
1 (14½ oz) can **diced tomatoes**, drained of juice
2½ pints hot **chicken stock**
salt and **black pepper**
bunch of **cilantro**, finely chopped

To serve
¼ cup **plain live yogurt**
French bread

Heat the ghee or oil in a heavy saucepan, stir in the onion, ginger, garlic, seeds, and sugar, and cook for 2 to 3 minutes. Add the carrots and cook for 2 minutes, stirring to coat well. Stir in the lentils, ras el hanout, tomatoes, and stock. Bring to a boil then reduce the heat and cook gently for about 20 minutes.

....

Season, stir in most of the chopped cilantro, and cook for another 5 minutes, or until the carrots and lentils are tender. Swirl a little of the yogurt into each portion, garnish with the remaining cilantro, and serve with some French bread.

....

CHICKEN MOLE

This rich Mexican chicken and chocolate dish is a treat—and it's bursting with powerful anti-aging nutrients.

Preparation time: 25 minutes
Cooking time: 1½ hours
Serves 4

....

3 tablespoons **vegetable oil**
1 (3lb) **chicken**, cut into 8 pieces
1 **onion**, chopped
1 **green bell pepper**, cored, seeded, and chopped
½ teaspoon **ground allspice**
½ teaspoon **ground cinnamon**
½ teaspoon **ground cumin**
1 teaspoon **chili powder**
2 **garlic cloves**, crushed
¾ cup canned **diced tomatoes**
1¼ cups **chicken stock**, divided
1 store-bought or homemade **corn tortilla**, torn into pieces, plus extra to serve (optional)
⅓ cup **blanched almonds**, coarsely chopped
2 tablespoons **sesame seeds**, plus extra for scattering
½ ounce **bittersweet chocolate**, coarsely chopped
salt and **black pepper**
chopped fresh **cilantro**, to garnish

Add the oil to a Dutch oven over medium heat and brown the chicken pieces for about 5 minutes, until golden on all sides. Transfer to a plate. Reduce the heat under the pot to low and add the onion and green bell pepper. Fry gently for 5 minutes, until softened, stirring in the spices and garlic for the last few minutes.

....

Add the tomatoes and half the stock and bring to a boil. Return the chicken to the pan, cover, and cook in a preheated oven, at 350°F, for 45 minutes.

....

Meanwhile, put the tortilla pieces into a food processor together with the almonds and sesame seeds. Blend until finely ground. Pour in the remaining stock and blend again until smooth. Stir the almond mixture and chocolate into the Dutch oven and return to the oven for 30 minutes, or until the chicken is cooked through and tender.

....

Season to taste with salt and black pepper, then scatter with extra sesame seeds and chopped cilantro to garnish. Serve with warmed tortillas, if using.

....

FENNEL-ROASTED LAMB WITH FIGS

Impressive enough for a dinner party, this has a cornucopia of vitamins and minerals to protect the body both inside and out.

Preparation time: 15 minutes
Cooking time: 25 minutes
Serves 4

3 **garlic cloves**, chopped
¼ cup peeled and chopped fresh **ginger root**
1 **red chile**, seeded and chopped
1 teaspoon **sea salt**
1 teaspoon **ground coriander**
1 teaspoon **ground cumin**
2 tablespoons **smen**, **ghee**, or softened **butter**
2 teaspoons **fennel seeds**
1½ lb lean loin of **lamb**
4 fresh **figs**, halved or quartered
2 tablespoons **honey**
salt and **black pepper**
small bunch of **cilantro**, finely chopped, to garnish
couscous, to serve (optional)

Using a mortar and pestle, pound the garlic, ginger, chile, and salt to form a coarse paste. Then add the ground spices. Beat the paste into the smen, ghee, or butter along with the fennel seeds.

Cut small incisions in the lamb and rub the mixture all over the meat, pressing it into the incisions. Put the lamb into a roasting pan and roast in a preheated oven, at 400°F, for 15 minutes.

Baste the lamb with the cooking juices, arrange the figs around it, and drizzle with honey. Season, then return it to the oven and cook for another 10 minutes or until cooked through. Garnish with the chopped cilantro and serve thickly sliced, with couscous, if using.

GUAVA-GLAZED PORK TENDERLOIN

Simply bursting with fruity, spicy flavor, this rejuvenating dish is full of powerful antioxidants to support your skin, bones, eyes, teeth, heart, and blood vessels.

Preparation time: 15 minutes, plus resting
Cooking time: 50 minutes
Serves 4

....

1 (2 lb) piece of **pork tenderloin**
finely grated zest and juice of 1 **lime**
1 tablespoon **olive oil**
1 teaspoon **honey**
sea salt and **black pepper**
7 oz mixed **fresh herbs** and **salad leaves**
⅓ cup **pomegranate seeds**

Guava glaze
1 tablespoon **olive oil**
1 small **onion**, diced
1 **garlic clove**, crushed
1 small **red chile**, seeded and diced
1 tablespoon **paprika**
2 teaspoons **ground coriander**
1 teaspoon **ground cinnamon**
1 teaspoon **ground ginger**
2 teaspoons **sea salt**
½ cup **guava juice**
finely grated zest and juice of 1 large **orange**
1 **guava**, peeled, seeded, and diced
1 tablespoon **apple cider vinegar**

For the glaze, heat the oil in a saucepan over low heat, add the onion, garlic clove, and chile and cook for 5 to 10 minutes or until the onion is soft. Add the remaining glaze ingredients, bring to a boil, then reduce the temperature and simmer for 20 minutes, stirring constantly, until the guava breaks down into the sauce and the sauce begins to thicken. Remove from the heat and brush half of the glaze over the pork tenderloin.

Transfer the pork tenderloin to a baking pan and place in a preheated oven, at 350°F, for 10 minutes. Brush with a little more of the glaze and return to the oven for 10 minutes or until just cooked through. Remove from the oven, pour over the remaining glaze, cover lightly with foil, and let rest for about 10 minutes.

In a salad bowl, whisk together the lime juice and zest, olive oil, and honey and season to taste. Sprinkle with the herbs and salad leaves, toss gently, then sprinkle with the pomegranate seeds. Slice the pork and serve with the salad on the side.

TOASTED QUINOA, TUNA & LENTIL SALAD

This delicious, savory, and satisfying salad is rich in omega-3 oils, protein, fiber, and antioxidants.

Preparation time: 20 minutes
Cooking time: 45 minutes
Serves 4

1 cup **quinoa**, rinsed and drained
2 tablespoons **olive oil,** divided
2 cups **vegetable stock**
5 oz **purple sprouting broccoli**, sliced
5 oz **asparagus** tips
1 cup fresh **peas**
3¾ cups shredded **collard greens**
1 small **red chile**, finely chopped
finely grated zest and juice of ½ **lemon**
1 **garlic clove**, crushed
4 fresh **tuna steaks**
1 (14 oz) can **Puy lentils**, rinsed and drained
8 **scallions**, diagonally sliced
handful of **mint** leaves, chopped
handful of **parsley**, chopped
3 tablespoons chopped **tarragon**
sea salt and **black pepper**

Dressing
finely grated zest and juice of 1 **lemon**
2 tablespoons **olive oil**
1 teaspoon **dried tarragon**
1 **garlic clove**, crushed

Put the quinoa in a large, nonstick saucepan over medium heat and stir until the water evaporates. Add half the olive oil and stir for another 15 minutes or until the quinoa begins to turn brown and pop. Add the stock and bring to a boil. Then reduce the heat and simmer for 20 minutes or until all the liquid has been absorbed and the quinoa is tender. Transfer to a large bowl and let cool.

Meanwhile, cook the broccoli, asparagus, peas, and collard greens in a large saucepan of lightly salted boiling water for about 2 to 3 minutes, then drain and plunge the vegetables into cold water. Drain and set aside. Make the dressing by whisking all the ingredients together in a small bowl.

Mix the chile, lemon zest and juice, and garlic in a small bowl and rub the mixture all over the tuna steaks. Season to taste and place under a preheated hot broiler for 3 minutes on each side, then transfer to a cutting board.

In a large salad bowl, toss the blanched vegetables, lentils, scallions, and herbs with the quinoa, stir in the dressing, and fluff up with a fork. Cut the tuna steaks into strips and set them on the salad. Grind a little black pepper over the top and serve.

ASPARAGUS & PEA QUINOA RISOTTO

Who says risotto needs rice? Protein-rich quinoa makes this a nutritious dish to preserve youthfulness and boost your health on all levels.

Preparation time: 5 minutes
Cooking time: 15 to 20 minutes
Serves 4

....

1⅔ cups **quinoa**, rinsed
2⅓ cups hot **vegetable stock**
8 oz **asparagus**, chopped
1⅓ cups **frozen peas**
1 tablespoon chopped **mint**
3 tablespoons grated
Parmesan cheese, divided
freshly ground **black pepper**

Put the quinoa and stock in a saucepan and bring to a boil. Then reduce the heat and simmer for about 12 to 15 minutes or until the quinoa is cooked, adding the asparagus and peas about 2 minutes before the end of the cooking time.

....

Drain the quinoa and vegetables, then return them to the pan with the mint and 2 tablespoons of the cheese. Season with black pepper and mix well.

....

Sprinkle with the remaining Parmesan cheese and serve.

....

MISO EGGPLANT WITH RICE NOODLES

Deep purple eggplant are a powerful source of age-busting vitamins and minerals to nourish you inside and out—brain, bones, skin, hair, and eyes.

Preparation time: 10 minutes
Cooking time: 15 minutes
Serves 4

....

12 **baby eggplants**, halved
¼ cup **white miso paste**
3 tablespoons **rice wine vinegar**
2 tablespoons **granulated sugar**
1 tablespoon **sake** or **water**
1 tablespoon **sesame seeds**
1 cup **edamame** (soybeans)
12 oz **rice noodles**, cooked
½ **cucumber**, thinly sliced
2 **scallions**, thinly sliced
salt

Make a crisscross pattern on the cut sides of the eggplant and place them, cut side down, on a broiler pan. Cook under a preheated hot broiler for 7 to 10 minutes, until charred.

Mix together the miso paste, 2 tablespoons of the rice wine vinegar, the sugar, and sake. Turn the eggplant over and brush over with the miso mixture. Return to the broiler for 3 to 5 minutes or until the eggplant halves are soft, then sprinkle with the sesame seeds and cook for another minute.

Meanwhile, cook the edamame beans in a saucepan of lightly salted boiling water for 2 minutes or until soft. Drain and cool under cold running water. Toss the beans together with the noodles, cucumber, scallions, and the remaining vinegar. Season with salt and serve with the broiled eggplant halves.

SESAME-CRUSTED TUNA WITH GINGER DRESSING

Zingy Asian flavors and omega-rich tuna: this can be served on its own or with steamed bok choy and some brown rice.

Preparation time: 15 minutes
Cooking time: 15 minutes
Serves 6

1 (1¾ lb) piece of **tuna**
salt and **black pepper**
2 tablespoons **vegetable oil**
3 tablespoons **white sesame seeds**
3 tablespoons **black sesame seeds**
½ **cucumber**, sliced into ribbons
2 **avocados**, sliced
2 **scallions**, shredded

Dressing
1 **garlic clove**, crushed
1 **chile**, seeded and diced
1 teaspoon finely chopped
fresh **ginger root**
1 tablespoon **soy sauce**
juice of ½ **lime**
1 teaspoon grated **orange zest**
1 tablespoon **honey**
1 tablespoon **sesame oil**

Season the tuna. Heat the vegetable oil in a large skillet, add the tuna, and cook for 3 to 5 minutes, or until browned all over. Scatter the sesame seeds evenly onto a plate and press the seared tuna into them until well coated. Cook in a preheated oven, at 425°F, for 10 to 12 minutes, or until browned but still pink inside.

Combine the ingredients for the dressing. Cut the tuna into thick slices and arrange on serving plates with the cucumber slices, avocados, and scallions. Drizzle with the dressing and serve.

TUNA WITH BELL PEPPERS & FENNEL GRATIN

Tuna, red bell peppers, and fennel are key anti-aging foods. This delicious meal will undoubtedly become a favorite standby.

Preparation time: 20 minutes, plus cooling
Cooking time: 45 minutes
Serves 4

4 **red bell peppers**
¼ cup **olive oil**
1 **garlic clove**, crushed
1 teaspoon **thyme** leaves
1 teaspoon chopped **basil**
1 teaspoon chopped **chives**
1 teaspoon **dried oregano**
sea salt and **black pepper**
4 fresh **tuna steaks**

Fennel gratin
3 large **fennel bulbs**, cut into wedges
2 **garlic cloves**, crushed
¼ teaspoon grated **nutmeg**
2 cups **heavy cream**
2 oz **Parmesan cheese**
2 oz **feta cheese**

Place the whole peppers under a preheated hot broiler for 10 to 15 minutes, turning from time to time, until black and blistered all over. Seal loosely in a plastic bag and set aside for 15 minutes, then peel off the skins. Remove the cores and seeds, cut the flesh into strips, and put them in a shallow bowl with 5 tablespoons of the oil, the garlic, and herbs. Season to taste and set aside.

Cook the fennel wedges in a large saucepan of lightly salted water for about 5 minutes, then remove them with a slotted spoon and transfer to a shallow baking dish. Add the garlic, nutmeg, and cream, season to taste, and stir to coat. Scatter with the Parmesan then crumble the feta on top. Grind over a little more black pepper and cook in a preheated oven, at 350°F, for 20 minutes or until golden and bubbling.

Brush the tuna steaks with the remaining olive oil and season to taste. Place under a preheated hot broiler for 2 to 3 minutes on each side until golden on the outside but still pink inside. Set aside to rest for a few minutes.

Arrange the marinated red bell peppers on 4 plates, slice the tuna, and arrange the slices on top. Serve with the fennel gratin.

BUTTERNUT, BROCCOLI & MUSHROOM GRATIN

Comfort food par excellence, with a boost of B vitamins and a range of antioxidants to make you look and feel younger.

Preparation time: 15 minutes
Cooking time: 15 minutes
Serves 4

....

8 oz **baby broccoli**, trimmed
2 cups peeled, seeded, and chopped
butternut squash
3 cups halved **mushrooms**
4 tablespoons **butter**
2 tablespoons **all-purpose flour**
1¾ cups **milk**
2 teaspoons **whole-grain mustard**
1 cup shredded **cheddar cheese**

Put the vegetables in a steamer and steam for 8 to 10 minutes or until tender. Transfer the vegetables to a baking dish.

....

Melt the butter in a small saucepan, then stir in the flour to make a roux. Cook for 1 to 2 minutes, then gradually whisk in the milk, and cook, stirring constantly, until the sauce is thick and smooth. Stir in the mustard and half the shredded cheese.

....

Pour the sauce over the vegetables and sprinkle with the remaining cheddar cheese. Cook under a preheated hot broiler for 5 to 6 minutes, until bubbling and golden.

....

CARAMELIZED GARLIC TART

A nod must go in the direction of chef Yotam Ottolenghi, whose recipe inspired this dish, with its big boost of anti-aging nutrients.

Preparation time: 20 minutes
Cooking time: 55 minutes
Serves 6 to 8

....

13 oz **store-bought puff pastry**
flour, for dusting
3 **garlic bulbs**, cloves separated
and peeled
1 **fennel bulb**, sliced
1 tablespoon **olive oil**
2 **red onions**, thinly sliced
1 tablespoon **balsamic vinegar**
1 cup **water**
1 tablespoon **superfine sugar**
1 teaspoon **rosemary** leaves, chopped
1 teaspoon **thyme** leaves
sea salt and **black pepper**
5 oz soft **goat cheese**, chopped
3½ oz **feta cheese**, chopped
2 oz **Parmesan cheese**, grated
2 **eggs**, lightly beaten
½ cup **heavy cream**
⅓ cup **Greek yogurt**

Roll out the puff pastry on a lightly floured surface to ⅜ inch thick and use it to line a greased 12-inch tart pan or pie plate. Cover with nonstick baking paper and pie weights and bake blind in a preheated oven, at 350°F, for 20 minutes. Remove the pie weights and paper and cook for another 5 minutes or until light brown.

....

Meanwhile, cook the garlic and fennel in a saucepan of boiling water for 3 to 4 minutes, then drain.

....

Heat the oil in a skillet over medium heat. Add the garlic, fennel, and onions. Fry for about 5 minutes or until the onions begin to soften. Add the vinegar and water and bring to a boil. Lower the heat and simmer, uncovered, for about 10 minutes. Stir in the sugar, rosemary, and thyme, season to taste, and cook, stirring frequently, until the vegetables are caramelized and the liquid has evaporated.

....

Dot the cheeses around the crust, then arrange the vegetables on top. Whisk the eggs, cream, and yogurt together until light and fluffy, season to taste, and pour over the cheese and vegetables. Return to the oven for 30 minutes or until the egg mixture has set and turned golden brown.

....

HEARTY RATATOUILLE

This one-pot meal is brimming with antioxidants and fiber to encourage overall health and well-being.

Preparation time: 15 minutes, plus salting
Cooking time: 1 hour to 1 hour 15 minutes
Serves 4

2 large **eggplant**
2 large **zucchini**
sea salt and **black pepper**
3 tablespoons **olive oil**
2 large **onions**, sliced
2 **red bell peppers**, cored, seeded, and cut into chunks
1 **fennel bulb**, cut into chunks
2 **garlic cloves**, crushed
1 (14 oz) can **cherry tomatoes** in juice
1 teaspoon **balsamic vinegar**
1 teaspoon **dried oregano**
handful of **basil**, torn

Cut the eggplant into chunks and slice the zucchini thickly, and put everything in a colander. Sprinkle with 1½ teaspoons of sea salt, toss to coat, then transfer to a clean dish towel. Wrap it tightly and set aside for 30 minutes to an hour.

Heat the olive oil in a Dutch oven over low heat and fry the onions for 5 to 10 minutes or until just soft. Add the red bell peppers, fennel chunks, and garlic cloves and cook for another 5 minutes. Squeeze the eggplant and zucchini in the dish towel to remove excess liquid, then add them to the pan.

Cook for a few minutes more, then add the cherry tomatoes, vinegar, and oregano. Cover and bring to a boil, then reduce the heat and simmer for about 45 minutes or until the tomatoes have broken down and the vegetables are tender.

Stir in half the basil and season to taste if necessary. Cook for another 10 to 15 minutes, uncovered, until the sauce is thick. Serve sprinkled with the remaining basil.

EGGPLANT, CHICKPEA & PANEER CURRY

This robust curry is quick and easy to make, and full of nutrients to reduce the impact of aging on all parts of your body.

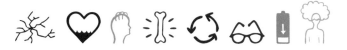

Preparation time: 20 minutes, plus salting
Cooking time: 45 minutes to 1 hour
Serves 4

1 large **eggplant**
sea salt and **black pepper**
1 tablespoon **olive oil**
2 **garlic cloves**, crushed
2 **onions**, chopped
3-inch piece of fresh **ginger root**, grated, plus extra to serve
1 teaspoon mild **chili powder**
1 teaspoon **ground cumin**
½ teaspoon **ground coriander**
½ teaspoon **ground turmeric**
½ teaspoon **garam masala**, plus extra to serve
2 (14 oz) cans **chickpeas**, rinsed and drained
¾ cup **coconut milk**
¼ cup **plain live yogurt**
handful of **mint** leaves, chopped
7 oz **paneer cheese**, cubed
3 oz fresh **cilantro**, chopped

Cut the eggplant into chunks and put in a colander. Sprinkle with 1½ teaspoons of sea salt and toss to coat. Transfer to a clean dish towel, wrap the towel tightly, and set aside for 30 minutes to an hour.

Heat the oil in a large saucepan or wok over low heat. Add the garlic, onions, and ginger. Cook for 10 minutes, stirring often, or until the onions are starting to caramelize. Squeeze the eggplant in the towel to remove excess liquid and add to the pan.

Add the chili powder, cumin, ground coriander, turmeric, and garam masala, and cook for another 2 to 3 minutes. Add the chickpeas and coconut milk, stir well, cover, and simmer for 20 to 30 minutes. Remove the lid and cook for another 10 minutes, mashing some of the chickpeas into the sauce to thicken.

Meanwhile, mix the yogurt in a bowl with the mint, season to taste, and set aside. Heat a nonstick skillet over medium heat, add the paneer, and cook briefly, stirring, until golden all over. Add the cheese to the curry, season if necessary, and add a pinch of garam masala, a grating of fresh ginger, and the fresh cilantro and toss to mix. Serve with the minty yogurt on the side.

SPAGHETTI WITH OLIVE OIL, GARLIC & CHILE

The simplicity of this dish belies the huge range of nutrients it contains. It's particularly good for skin, hair, and joints.

Preparation time: 5 minutes
Cooking time: 10 to 15 minutes
Serves 4

13 oz **wholewheat spaghetti**
½ cup **olive oil**
4 **garlic cloves**, minced
2 small **red chiles**, seeded and finely chopped
sea salt and **black pepper**
handful of **parsley**, chopped, to garnish
grated **pecorino cheese**, to serve (optional)

Cook the spaghetti in a large saucepan of lightly salted boiling water or according to package instructions until al dente.

Heat the oil in a large, heavy skillet over low heat and add the garlic cloves and chile. Cook gently for 1 to 2 minutes or until the garlic just starts to turn golden.

Drain the pasta and transfer to the skillet with about 3 tablespoons of the cooking water. Season to taste and toss to coat the pasta in the oil. Transfer to a dish, sprinkle with parsley, and serve with grated pecorino cheese, if using.

BAKED HONEY, CARDAMOM & CINNAMON FIGS

Cinnamon is known for its beneficial effect on joints, but did you know it also aids digestion, circulation, and bone health?

Preparation time: 5 minutes
Cooking time: 25 minutes
Serves 4

12 ripe **fresh figs**
1 tablespoon **ghee** or **butter**,
plus extra for greasing
grated zest of 1 **lemon**
¼ cup **honey**
2 teaspoons **cardamom seeds**
2 **cinnamon sticks**
yogurt, **crème fraîche**,
or **heavy cream**, to serve
powdered sugar, for dusting

Cut each of the figs lengthwise into quarters, keeping the bottom intact, and place in a lightly greased baking dish.

Melt the ghee or butter in a small saucepan, stir in the lemon zest, honey, cardamom seeds, and cinnamon sticks, and cook for 2 minutes, until bubbling. Pour the mixture evenly over the figs.

Bake in a preheated oven, at 400°F, for 20 minutes. Dust with powdered sugar and serve accompanied by yogurt, crème fraîche, or heavy cream for spooning into the middle of each fig.

FRUIT SALSA & CINNAMON TRIANGLES

This delicious, light dessert is full of antioxidants to boost the health and well-being of the whole family.

Preparation time: 15 minutes, plus cooling
Cooking time: 10 minutes
Serves 4
....

1 **kiwifruit**, peeled and diced
⅔ cup **blackberries**, halved
⅔ cup **strawberries**, hulled and sliced
⅔ cup **raspberries**, halved
1 **Pink Lady apple**, cored and diced
1 **pear**, cored and diced
⅓ cup **pomegranate seeds**
1 tablespoon **pomegranate molasses**
finely grated zest and juice of 1 **orange**
1 teaspoon **ground cinnamon**
½ teaspoon **ground ginger**
2 tablespoons **honey**
3 tablespoons chopped **mint**

Cinnamon triangles
1 tablespoon **olive oil**
1 teaspoon **ground cinnamon**
1 tablespoon **honey**
2 soft **whole-wheat tortillas**

Combine all the fruit salsa ingredients in a large bowl. Cover and let stand so that the flavors can blend.
....

For the cinnamon triangles, whisk together the oil, cinnamon, and honey and brush the mixture over both sides of the tortillas. Use a sharp knife or a pizza wheel and cut the tortillas into triangles, then arrange them on a cookie sheet and bake in a preheated oven, at 350°F for about 10 minutes or until just crisp. Let cool.
....

Serve the salsa in a big dipping dish or in individual ramekins, with the cinnamon triangles on the side.
....

Leftover salsa can be stored in an airtight container in the refrigerator for up to 4 days.
....

MOLTEN CHOCOLATE LAVA CAKES

A sumptuous dark-chocolate dessert, this dish will improve your mood, while also helping your skin, teeth, hair, heart, and brain.

Preparation time: 10 minutes
Cooking time: 25 minutes
Serves 2

6 tablespoons **butter**, plus extra
for greasing
⅓ cup **superfine sugar**
3 oz **semisweet chocolate**, broken
into pieces
2 medium **eggs**
3 tablespoons **all-purpose flour**

To serve
cream
raspberries

Grease 2 individual ovenproof ramekins and sprinkle with 1 teaspoon of the sugar.

Melt together the chocolate and butter in a microwave-safe bowl in a microwave on medium, checking on it every minute until melted and smooth.

Whisk together the eggs and remaining sugar using a handheld stick blender or in a stand mixer until thick, pale, and creamy. Beat in the melted chocolate mixture, then lightly fold in the flour.

Spoon the mixture into the two prepared ramekins and place on a baking pan. Bake the cakes in a preheated oven, at 375°F, for 15 to 20 minutes or until firm on the outside but still wobbly in the center.

Turn out the cakes into 2 serving bowls and serve warm with cream and raspberries.

BANANAS WITH SPICED CHOCOLATE

The resveratrol in dark chocolate, the polyphenols in cinnamon, and the B vitamins in the bananas put anti-aging power into this decadent dessert.

Preparation time: 5 minutes
Cooking time: 5 minutes
Serves 4

4 ripe **bananas**, sliced lengthwise
butter, for greasing
1 teaspoon **ground allspice**
½ teaspoon **ground nutmeg**
juice of 1 **lemon**
½ cup slivered **almonds**
1 cup **Greek** or **plain live yogurt**
3 walnut-sized pieces of **crystalized ginger**, diced

Place the banana slices in a lightly buttered baking dish. Sprinkle with the spices and lemon juice.

Bake them in a preheated oven, at 350°F, for 12 to 15 minutes.

Meanwhile, mix together the yogurt and preserved ginger in a bowl.

Divide the bananas among 4 dessert dishes, add spoonfuls of yogurt, and drizzle with the spiced chocolate. Sprinkle with the slivered almonds to serve.

CRANBERRY ICE CREAM WITH DARK CHOCOLATE

This mouthwatering dessert is packed with loads of antioxidants, calcium, and a range of nutrients to rejuvenate and uplift.

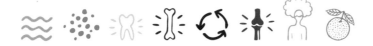

Preparation time: 10 minutes, plus cooling and freezing
Cooking time: 15 minutes
Serves 6

3⅔ cups **cranberries**
⅓ cup **water**
1 teaspoon **ground cinnamon**
¾ cup **demerara sugar**
seeds scraped from 1 **vanilla bean**
2½ cups **heavy whipping cream**
1 cup **plain live yogurt**
⅓ cup **dark chocolate chips**

Put the cranberries, water, cinnamon, and one-third of the sugar in a saucepan over medium heat. Bring to a boil, reduce the heat, cover, and cook for about 10 minutes or until the cranberries have softened into the liquid. Let cool for 20 minutes, mashing the fruit with a fork.

Put the cranberry mixture in a food processor and pulse until coarsely chopped.

Put the remaining sugar, the vanilla seeds, whipping cream, and live yogurt in a heavy saucepan over medium heat. Stir until the sugar has completely dissolved, then stir in the cranberry mixture to combine.

Transfer to a shallow dish and place in the freezer for about 1 hour. Stir in the chocolate chips and freeze again for another hour, or until softly set.

GUAVA ICE CREAM
WITH BLACKBERRY COULIS

This is an easy recipe that can be prepared in advance to supply a burst of fiber, antioxidants, and vitamins to turn back the clock.

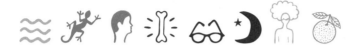

Preparation time: 10 minutes, plus freezing
Cooking time: 20 minutes
Serves 4 to 6

....

6 ripe **guavas**, peeled, seeded, and diced
½ cup **demerara sugar**
finely grated zest and juice of 1 **lime**
2½ cups **whipping cream**
1 teaspoon **vanilla extract**

Coulis
1⅓ cups **blackberries**
2 tablespoons **honey**
¼ cup **water**

Put the guava, sugar, and lime zest and juice in a shallow dish and place in the freezer for about 2 hours, or until just frozen.

....

Meanwhile, put the blackberries, honey, and water in a small, heavy saucepan over medium heat. Bring to a boil, then reduce the heat and simmer, mashing the berries into the liquid from time to time, for about 15 minutes, or until thick. The purée can be strained if desired, but the seeds are also rich in nutrients. Let cool.

....

Beat the cream and vanilla extract using a stand mixer until the mixture forms soft peaks. Add the frozen guava mixture and blend until smooth. Serve immediately with the coulis, or store in an airtight container in the freezer until ready to serve.

....

POMEGRANATE PANNA COTTA

This super dessert is easy to make and is rich in calcium and anti-aging antioxidants to keep your bones strong and your skin, hair, and mood glowing.

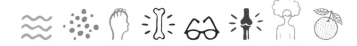

Preparation time: 10 minutes, plus chilling
Cooking time: 5 minutes
Serves 6

4 sheets of **gelatin**
1 **vanilla bean**, split lengthwise
2½ cups **heavy cream**
1 cup **skim milk**
1 cup **demerara sugar**
⅓ cup **pomegranate seeds**, plus extra to decorate
finely grated zest of ½ **orange**
2 tablespoons **pomegranate molasses**
2 tablespoons **orange juice**
mint leaves, to decorate

Soak the gelatin in a cup of cold water for about 5 minutes or until softened.

Scrape the seeds out of the vanilla bean and place in a large, heavy saucepan with the vanilla bean, cream, milk, and sugar. Bring to a boil over medium heat, stirring constantly until the sugar has dissolved. Remove from the heat and lift out and discard the vanilla bean.

Squeeze the gelatin sheets to remove any excess water, then add to the pan, one by one, and stir until dissolved.

Wet the insides of 6 large ramekins with cold water and set aside. Mix the pomegranate seeds and orange zest in a small bowl and spoon the mixture into the the ramekins. Pour in the vanilla cream and let chill in the refrigerator for 2 to 3 hours or until set.

To serve, dip the base of each ramekin in hot water for a few seconds, then turn out the panna cottas onto plates. Whisk the pomegranate molasses with the orange juice and drizzle it over the top of each sering. Sprinkle with extra pomegranate seeds and decorate with mint.

BLACKBERRY BRÛLÉES

These divine little pots, with all the nutrient power of shiny purple blackberries, are quick to prepare and delicious to eat.

Preparation time: 5 minutes, plus cooling
Cooking time: 5 minutes
Serves 4

1½ cups **blackberries**
2 tablespoons **apple juice**
2 to 3 teaspoons **superfine sugar**,
to taste
½ cup **Greek yogurt**
2 tablespoons firmly packed
dark **brown sugar**

Put the blackberries, apple juice, and sugar in a saucepan and simmer for 2 to 3 minutes. Spoon into 4 individual ramekins and let cool for 2 to 3 minutes.

Spoon the yogurt over the berries then, sprinkle brown sugar on each serving.

Cover and chill until required.

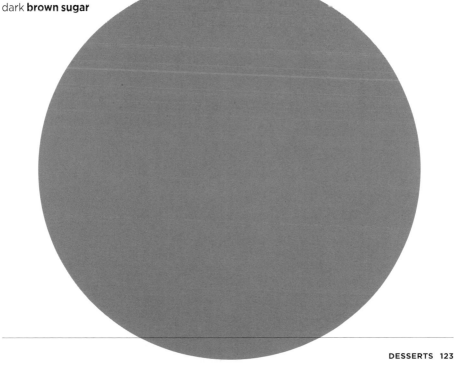

APPLE & BLACKBERRY COMPOTE WITH ALMOND SCONES

A lovely autumnal dish with all the antioxidant goodness of apples and blackberries, and vitamin E from the almonds.

Preparation time: 20 minutes
Cooking time: 15 minutes
Serves 4

....

3 Granny Smith or other cooking **apples**, peeled, cored, and sliced
2 tablespoons **water**
1 cup **blackberries**
2 tablespoons **apricot jam**
crème fraîche or other thick cream, to serve

Scones
1 cup **all-purpose flour**, plus extra for dusting
1 teaspoon **baking powder**
½ cup **ground almonds**
⅓ cup **superfine sugar**
4 tablespoons **butter**
⅓ cup **milk**, plus extra for brushing
1 teaspoon **vanilla extract**
¼ cup slivered **almonds**

To make the scones, sift the flour, baking powder, ground almonds, and sugar into a food processor. Add the butter and pulse to make fine crumbs. Add the milk and vanilla extract and pulse to make a soft dough. Turn out the dough onto a floured surface and lightly knead. Press the dough out with your fingers, then stamp out 8 circles using a 3-inch fluted round cookie cutter.

....

Place on a nonstick cookie sheet, brush with a little milk, and decorate with the slivered almonds. Bake in a preheated oven, at 400°F, for 10 to 15 minutes or until golden.

....

Meanwhile, put the apples into a saucepan over medium heat. Add the water and cook for about 3 minutes or until soft. Stir in the blackberries and apricot preserves and simmer for 1 minute.

....

Spoon the compote into 4 shallow bowls, with 2 scones along the side of each, and serve with crème fraiche.

....

RESOURCES

American Academy of Ophthalmology
Tel: (415) 447-0213
Email: eyesmart@aao.org
Website: www.geteyesmart.org

American Chronic Pain Association
Tel: (800) 533-3231
Website: www.theacpa.org

American Heart Association
Tel: (800) 242-8721
Website: www.heart.org

The American Institute of Stress
Tel: (682) 239-6823
Email: info@stress.org
Website: www.stress.org

American Meditation Society
Website: americanmeditationsociety.org

American Nutrition Association
Website: americannutritionassociation.org

American Yoga Association
Email: info@americanyogaassociation.org
Website: americanyogaassociation.org

**Anxiety and Depression Association
of America**
Tel: (240) 485-1001
Website: www.adaa.org

Arthritis Foundation
Tel: (404) 872-7100
Website: www.arthritis.org

Brain & Behavior Research Foundation
Tel: (800) 829-8289
Website: www.bbrfoundation.org

Diabetes Action
Tel: (202) 333-4520
Email: info@diabetesaction.org
Website: www.diabetesaction.org

Insomnia Land
Website: www.insomnialand.com

Mayo Clinic
Website: www.mayoclinic.org/healthy-living/
stress-management/resources/HLV-20049495

Mental Health and Addiction Network
Tel: (617) 949-0030
Website: www.mhfederation.org

**Mouth Healthy (sponsored by the American
Dental Association)**
Website: www.mouthhealthy.org

National Council on Aging
Helpline: (202) 479-1200
Website: www.ncoa.org

National Osteoporosis Foundation
Tel: (800) 231-4222
Website: www.nof.org

The Obesity Society
Tel: (301) 563-6526
Website: www.obesity.org

INDEX

Almonds
  apple & blackberry
    compote with
    almond scones 124
  chicken mole 92
apples
  apple & blackberry
    compote with
    almond scones 124
asparagus & pea quinoa
  risotto 99
avocados 23
  avocado & sardine
    salad with zesty
    dressing 72
  avocado & tomato
    tostados 60
  baked avocado egg
    cups 44
  chilled avocado
    soup 90

Bananas
  banana, oat & black-
    berry muffins 68
  bananas with spiced
    chocolate 116
  guava & ginger
    smoothie 38
beets
  carrot & beet
    tabbouleh 78
bell peppers
  broccoli & red
    pepper frittata 46
  gazpacho 83
  hearty ratatouille 108
  huevos rancheros 48
  Mediterranean stuffed
    bell peppers 82
  red bell peppers 15
  tuna with bell peppers
    & fennel gratin 104
berries
  berry & Brazil nut

    smoothie 39
  berry & coconut
    oatmeal 43
blackberries 21
  apple & blackberry
    compote with
    almond scones 124
  banana, oat & black-
    berry muffins 68
  blackberry brûlées 125
  fruit salsa & cinnamon
    triangles 114
  guava ice cream with
    blackberry coulis 120
blueberry pomegranate
  smoothie 36
Brazil nuts 12
  berry & Brazil nut
    smoothie 39
  fruit & nut muesli 42
  spicy Brazil nuts 56
broccoli 21
  broccoli & red
    pepper frittata 46
  broccoli salad with dill
    & pine nuts 76
  butternut, broccoli &
    mushroom gratin 105
  pesto broccoli with
    poached eggs 80
bruschetta with
  tomatoes & basil 62
bulgur wheat
  carrot & beet
    tabbouleh 78
butternut, broccoli &
  mushroom gratin 105

Carrots 18
  carrot & beet
    tabbouleh 78
  carrot & lentil
    muffins 66
  carrot & Puy lentil
    salad 75

  carrot, cilantro & lentil
    soup 91
  carrot chips with
    honey yogurt dip 58
cheese
  caramelized garlic
    tart 106
  eggplant, chickpea &
    paneer curry 110
  Greek feta & mint
    dip 52
  Mediterranean stuffed
    bell peppers 82
  watercress soup
    with cheese and oat
    crackers 88
chicken mole 92
chickpeas
  eggplant, chickpea &
    paneer curry 110
chiles
  roasted chile & lemon
    sardines 84
  spaghetti with olive
    oil, garlic & chile 111
chocolate
  bananas with spiced
    chocolate 116
  chicken mole 92
  cranberry ice cream
    with dark
    chocolate 118
  dark chocolate 22
  molten chocolate lava
    cakes 115
coconut
  berry & coconut
    oatmeal 43
cranberries 13
  cranberry ice cream
    with dark
    chocolate 118
  cranberry muffins 69
  spiced raisin &
    cranberry cookies 64

Eggplant 14
  eggplant & sesame
    noodle salad 70
  eggplant, chickpea &
    paneer curry 110
  hearty ratatouille 108
  miso eggplant with
    rice noodles 100
  smoky eggplant dip 53
eggs 25
  aïoli with crispbreads
    & crudités 54
  baked avocado egg
    cups 44
  broccoli & red
    pepper frittata 46
  huevos rancheros 48
  pesto broccoli with
    poached eggs 80
  poached eggs on
    quinoa hash
    browns 49

Fennel 18-9
  caramelized garlic
    tart 106
  fennel & cumin
    Waldorf salad 74
  fennel & mushroom
    tarts 86
  fennel-roasted lamb
    with figs 94
  tuna with bell peppers
    & fennel gratin 104
figs
  baked honey,
    cardamom &
    cinnamon figs 112
  fennel-roasted lamb
    with figs 94
  fruit salsa & cinnamon
    triangles 114

Garlic 24
  aïoli with crispbreads

& crudités 54
caramelized garlic
tart 106
spaghetti with olive
oil, garlic & chile 111
gazpacho 83
guavas 23
guava & ginger
smoothie 38
guava & mango
shake 57
guava ice cream with
blackberry coulis 120
guava-glazed pork
tenderloin 96

Hearty ratatouille 108

Ice cream
cranberry ice cream
with dark
chocolate 118
guava ice cream with
blackberry coulis 120

Lamb
fennel-roasted lamb
with figs 94
lentils
carrot & lentil
muffins 66
carrot & Puy lentil
salad 75
carrot, cilantro & lentil
soup 91
toasted quinoa, tuna
& lentil salad 98

Mangoes
guava & mango
shake 57
Mediterranean stuffed
bell peppers 82

miso eggplant with rice
noodles 100
mushrooms
butternut, broccoli &
mushroom gratin 105
fennel & mushroom
tarts 86

Noodles
eggplant & sesame
noodle salad 70
miso eggplant with
rice noodles 100

Oats 19
banana, oat & black-
berry muffins 68
fruit & nut muesli 42
on-the-go granola
bars 40
rosemary oat
crackers 63
spiced raisin &
cranberry cookies 64
watercress soup with
cheese and oat
crackers 88
olive oil 14
olives
citrus olives 50
Greek feta & mint
dip 52
oranges
citrus olives 50
pomegranate panna
cotta 122

Peas
asparagus & pea
quinoa risotto 99
pesto broccoli with
poached eggs 80
pomegranates 16

blueberry pomegranate
smoothie 36
pomegranate panna
cotta 122
pork
guava-glazed pork
tenderloin 96

Quinoa 24
asparagus & pea
quinoa risotto 99
Mediterranean stuffed
bell peppers 82
poached eggs on
quinoa hash
browns 49
toasted quinoa, tuna
& lentil salad 98

Rosemary oat
crackers 63
Sardines 22
avocado & sardine
salad with zesty
dressing 72
roasted chile & lemon
sardines 84
sesame-crusted tuna
with ginger
dressing 102
spaghetti with olive oil,
garlic & chile 111

Tomatoes 16
avocado & tomato
tostados 60
bruschetta with
tomatoes & basil 62
huevos rancheros 48
tuna 13
sesame-crusted tuna
with ginger
dressing 102

toasted quinoa, tuna
& lentil salad 98
tuna with bell peppers
& fennel gratin 104

Watercress 17
watercress soup with
cheese and oat
crackers 88

ACKNOWLEDGMENTS

Thinkstock Alexander Kovalchuk 20; Frans Rombout 7; gemenacom 30; Hemera Technologies 12; Jovan Nikolic 8; Natikka 17; pattymalajak 9; sommail 28; Wavebreakmedia Ltd 27.